the Spinning Wheel

The Art of Mythmaking

the Spinning Wheel

The Art of Mythmaking

by
Gwendolyn Endicott

Cover Illustration
Marz Eve

Design
Michael Brugman

Attic
press

1907 SE 39th
Portland, Oregon 97214
(503) 368-6389

Printed by Ecoprint, a printer located in Portland, Oregon specializing in
environmentally responsible printing.

Cover printed on 100% post-consumer recycled paper. Inside pages printed on 50% recycled paper,
with a minimum of 10% post-consumer waste. Entire book printed with non-petroleum-based soy inks.
The cover has not been laminated because of the toxic byproducts released into the environment
from the lamination process.

Special Thanks

to Laura Brugman for endless hours imputing *The Spinning Wheel* on computer and for her constant support and encouragement,

to graphic designer, Michael Brugman, for taking this project as his own in designing the layout of the book,

to Waverly Fitzgerald for giving me permission to tell my own stories,

to artist Marz Eve, whose drawing of The Ancestor gives this book its face,

to Pat Hollister for researching and editorial assistance,

to Rhia for her belief that anything is possible,

and to my students for the continual gift of inspiration.

Contents

movement one

LOOKING AT THE FACES OF SELF 1

Think of this movement as a House of Mirrors. As you look into the mirrors, you will see the faces of your self. These are the masks of your identity, or in psychological terms, your "persona." You will see in these mirrors some of the major archetypes of your growth.

movement two

MAPPING YOUR PATHWAYS OF GROWTH..................15

In this movement, think of yourself as a map maker, charting your lands of experience, tracing your pathways of growth. You will use the "eagle's-eye" view, that allows you to see from a distance, to see from the sky. With this ability, comes understanding of your life territory.

movement three

FINDING THE CENTER PLACE 31

Think of this movement as an invitation to a reunion. You are asked to go back "home" again. Like concentric bowls, fitting one inside the other — home is your seed essence, home is your habitat, home is your planet, home is your spiral galaxy. When you journey back home, you go to the wellspring of your power.

movement four

RECEIVING THE GIFTS OF FEMININE WISDOM........................47

In this movement, imagine yourself visiting a fountain whose waters break through the surface of time and are called "memory." From this fountain, you can collect the many gifts of your life experience. From these waters, you can re-collect the gifts of your ancestral, cultural, and planetary heritage. It is here that you become a keeper of the story.

Contents

movement five

In this movement, you receive the gifts of imagination. Think of them as "possibilities." Imagine that you are holding a cornucopia of overflowing abundance. In this cornucopia, you see the animals, the plants, the people; the mountains and rivers and oceans — the living planet. In it you can also see all of your own potential, your own possibilities.

movement six

In this movement, you journey into the depths of a magical mountain. Weather moves and changes around the mountain: clouds and mists and sun; moon and stars and storm. Inside the mountain is the well of time beyond measure that some call Dream-Time — the realm of vision and dream, the realm of ancestral wisdom. To enter here, follow the sound of your own soul birthing. This birthing call leads you deeper, through the passages of self to the central chamber where old gives birth to the new.

movement seven

In this movement, imagine that you enter a giant astro-dome where you stand surrounded by the universe. Galaxies and solar systems, planets and stars turn in their cycles around you. So clearly do you perceive them that you even hear the sound of their changing — the expansion, the contraction, the cyclic turning, the rhythmic balance. As the sound grows, you hear it inside you — a pulse, a rhythm, as familiar as in-tide and out-tide, as familiar as your breath or the beat of your heart.

Introduction

Once I stood among a small crowd of people watching an artist paint. "How long did it take you to paint that picture," the man next to me asked, pointing to a finished landscape. The silence was long. I remember feeling uncomfortable, thinking it a wrong question. "All my life," the artist quietly replied. I knew the answer was true.

The Spinning Wheel is a teaching book that grows from almost forty years of teaching experience. That a book has grown from my teaching is somewhat surprising to me — for it is the act of teaching itself (rather than writing) that excites me. I love to create the opportunity — the environment, the assignment, the exercise, the suggestion — that leads people into new discovery. I like the aliveness of people who are opening, who are growing. I think of teaching as a kind of magic — the magic of bringing potential forward. I have, only half kiddingly, told my friend and editor, Waverly Fitzgerald, that after I die, my mind will probably still be spinning out journal exercises for angels willing to listen.

I am hoping that claiming this forty years of teaching will give me the foundation for a confession. What I most like to teach is what I am in the process of learning. That is the tip of the wave, where the excitment of the new dances. From this place, come the teaching approaches of *The Spinning Wheel,* and from this place, come my own learning stories.

Several years after I began teaching college classes in mythology, I discovered that I had begun to use it, much like a language, to describe my own life and growth. But that wasn't all. I also realized that I had found a soul language, a way of speaking to a very deep place in myself — and a way of giving that place a voice to speak. A part of me that had been mute for many years began to open and grow.

I began to teach mythology as a language in what I called Spinning Wheel classes; these were circle classes where we wove our personal mythologies. In one of the books I love most, *Daughters of Copperwoman,* Anne Cameron tells us that a story belongs to the one telling it, and that we betray the trust of others, in this case, the native people of Vancouver Island, if we appropriate their stories and retell them. Look instead, she says, into your own story. "Search for it; then write it, sing it, paint it, dance it, and share it." In the Spinning Wheel classes, we searched, we wrote, we sang, we painted, we danced — and we shared the incredible variety of stories that emerged.

These circles met in the attic of a huge old frame house; three stories below cars whooshed by in the busy city street. I jokingly told the circle that we were already part of archetypal mythology for there we were, in the attic, working at the spinning wheel, spinsters spinning the threads, weaving the patterns. These circles inspired the exercises and approaches of this book.

On the evening of the first of these classes, I threw the runes as I often do at the beginning of something new. Moving my hand over the smooth white stones, I turned up one. It was the rune "Sowelu," meaning Wholeness. It was the same rune I had turned months earlier when I first conceived the idea for this class. Once more I read "...what you are striving to become in actuality is what you already are in essence; it is your *personal myth,* that which you are to make conscious, bring into form, express in a creative way." To this day, these words still best express my understanding of this work.

For years now, my teaching philosophy has been "don't just talk about it, show them." The exercises in this book are created to show you how to bring into form your personal myth.

gwendolyn Endicott
February 1993

Acknowledgement

The title of this book, *The Spinning Wheel*, and many of its teachings were given to me by an ancient Grand Mother. I see her frequently in the rainforest where I live on the Oregon Coast. On Autumn mornings, when I take my early morning walk, I notice she has been there already. The forest has been spun. Everywhere I look — flashes of rainbow light. Silken wheels spun on filamental threads between cedar and spruce, fern and huckleberry. The breeze blows them like the morning's spider laundry — cloaks of many sizes turning silken in the air. At night, I see her nested into her white cloak, sitting silent in the ceiling corners of the shed where I sleep.

Some say she is the Oldest One — she who weaves the fabric of creation from the center of herself; she who looking into the rich dark abyss yearns form into being.

Spider Woman, say the Hopi, seeing the silent, empty earth, desired that joy be born. Mixing earth with the water of her mouth, she sang forth the first beings, weaving, weaving for them a fine cloak of rainbow filament; singing, singing into the fabric of its design the songs of knowledge, the songs of wisdom, the songs of love. And twins came forth — dancing female, dancing male; they who began the preparing of a human world, forming it beautiful, forming it harmonious, filling it with songs of joy.

Do not forget, the people were told; sing, sing praises to creation, sing joy in living. And so singing, may the tops of your heads stay open to the joyous filaments of your connection to the center, to the self from which you spin.

Four times the people forgot; four times the people fought; four times they spun out destruction; four times the earth was destroyed, and three times spun again.[1]

• • •

Spider, says Barbara Walker, was a totemic form of the fate-spinner. "The spider's web was likened to the Wheel of Fate and the spider to the Goddess as a spinner, sitting at the hub of her wheel."[2] Spider reminds us that we, too, are weavers — weavers of the fabric of our lives. She reminds us of the power of our desiring and that out of this desiring we create possibilities. Remembering her songs of joy and wisdom, remembering the power of our own voices to sing, we spin our stories — making the connections, re-membering the beauty; at the same time knowing that to complete the design, some threads must be cut, some creations destroyed.

She spins, she weaves, she repairs, she chooses, she shapes and she cuts. She creates. She destroys. As do these human hands of mine. As does this human mind of mine.

This mandala of Spider the Creatress, carved on shell, was found
in a burial mound in Oklahoma. It is a "gorget," a throat shield, that
was worn by native women around 1300 C.E. One might imagine
the creative power of voice that such a shield evoked.

You Are The Weaver

SOME SUGGESTIONS ON USING THIS BOOK

The language of mythology works through images and the play of those images on the imagination. It is as old as the drawings on cave walls and as new as the spinning of your dreams and stories. The approach of this book is to describe an image through story and myth, then to suggest ways of allowing it to unfold your personal story.

Give your responses total latitude; no one is critiquing, editing, or judging you. Expression may take many forms—words, drawings, colors, abstract shapes, dialogues. It is important to allow whatever wants to come out. Try not to let your mind censor. The mind is good at this and tricky: "I never could draw," "I can't express it," "this is too hard," "it's not important," "I shouldn't feel this way," and so on and on.

Dwell with the images. When you cultivate a language like mythology that speaks to the deep self, responses, images, ideas may come at any time or in any place—while sleeping, while riding the bus, while planting potatoes, while making love. Still, it is important to allow yourself time and space for this process. Interruptions, (or the fear of interruptions) keep you on the surface of things. Ideally, give yourself time in a space where both the body and the mind feel safe and comfortable.

As you set about remembering and re-weaving your life territory, emotions surface. A gifted psychic teacher, Mark Wallek, once told me: "Emotion is energy in motion." Emotion is your aliveness, your sensitivity to experience. When emotion is moving, something is happening. Many have been taught to stifle emotion in order to stay in control. When we do this, we lose touch with our sensitivity; we have no way to relate to our emotions and the emotions of others without feeling overwhelmed. At the end of the book, you will find a section, "Surfing Emotion," that gives you some practical ways of working with emotion.

Although the material of this book may be an individual journey, it comes alive easily in circle. The section "For Circles," also at the end of the book, contains some of the games and rituals I have created while working with this material in circles. Both play and ritual bring the abstract into personal experience and touch the spirit more intimately than words.

I think you will get the most out of *The Spinning Wheel* if you move slowly through the sequence of images, letting your curiosity and desire lead you to the approaches you want to try. Take your time with each. When I work in circle classes with the material, we sometimes dwell for several weeks with one image, letting it unfold. And then, we may move on to a new focus, but that image is still working not only in our unconscious but in our imagination. It has become part of our "vocabulary."

I would suggest going through the entire sequence of seven chapters first (I think of them as movements) before skipping around in the book. Not only do the mythic images interrelate, but they build upon one another. The book, itself, moves in a spiral: Movements One and Two "spin out" through identity and journey; Movements Three and Four spin back in, toward center and integration of experience; Movement Five spins out again by attracting new possibilties; Movement Six spins inward more deeply to the place of dreaming and renewing; and Movement Seven turns the wheel of balance in this growing cycle.

The book is both a "spinning-wheel" and a "spinning wheel" just as mythology is a language that describes growth (shows its design) and also evokes growth. The image of growth as a spiral is part of what I call "spider mythology": spinning out from center, back to center; out from center, back to center.

The graphics that introduce an image sequence follow this pattern:

 WEB: my telling of mythic story, both historical and personal.

 HANDS: an exercise of creative expression, the weaving of your personal mythology.

 WINGS: an exercise for the stirring of an image in your imagination.

grand mother

GRANDMOTHER, *where do I begin? What thread begins the yarn? What story begins the weave?*

Begin with the stirring, begin with the stirring in your own dark center, begin...

MOVEMENT 1

Looking At
The Faces of Self

There was a child went forth every day,
And the first object he looked upon and received with wonder
    or pity or love or dread, that object he became.
And that object became part of him for the day or a certain
    part of the day... or for many years or stretching cycles of years.

The early lilacs became part of this child.
And grass, and white and red morningglories, and white and red clover, and the
    song of the phoebe bird,
And the March-born lambs, and the sow's pink-faint litter, and the mare's foal
    and the cow's calf, and the noisy brood of the barnyard or by the mire of the
    pond-side... and the fish suspending themselves so curiously below there...
    and the beautiful curious liquid... and the water plants with their graceful
    flat heads... all became part of him
      from *There Was a Child Went Forth*, Walt Whitman

 ## THERE WAS A CHILD WENT FORTH...

And that child was me. I remember the faces that were me. These — and many more: two year old round, soft girl baby asleep on a beach, cuddled, arms around the family dog — the two warmly nestled, sleeping, perhaps dreaming, together. The skinny girl of seven, in the photo wearing a red taffeta pinafore, shyly looking out from behind herself, the girl with the skinned up knees, who climbed trees and knew how they felt in her hands, but who was confused by people and never knew what to say. The Christmas picture of a young woman, wearing a brown wool dress chosen by her husband, smiling, arms around her toddler son and infant daughter. The grey haired woman, legs strong with walking and working, hair wild, standing tall by a rainforest thistle that towers above her. She is surrounded by green, this woman who has fallen in love with a rainforest. In the face of the woman, standing amid the rainforest, I still see the essence of her, that child who went forth so many years ago.

There is a word that describes the ability we have to create identity and to change identity as we grow. The word is persona. Sometimes it is defined literally as "mask." As actors in our living, we create our masks as we grow and change, and we destroy our masks when they no longer work for us, or when circumstance forces us to change. Sometimes change happens so fast, like a structure crumbling or perhaps even exploding, that we are left for awhile with the feeling of having no persona. This can be an intensely uncomfortable and vulnerable experience, much like having no clothes. One woman who had always thought of herself as shy and "just ordinary" found she was more and more in positions of influence and power. People respected her ability. Many saw her as an authority. Although she had outgrown her old way of seeing herself, she had not yet found her "new clothes." She told of a dream where she wandered through a building with many rooms, looking for a pair of shoes that fit her. She was willing to steal them for she had no shoes. She also needed a new dress, but the one she found was not sewed on either side; the front and back were not connected. She could see them flying separately away from her body as she walked.

When, in time, we have become again comfortable in our new "clothes," we have a tendency to look back and wonder: how could I have thought that, been that, done that? The old persona has become a cast off mask.

I like to think of persona as the growing edge: the way I am unfolding at the moment. Looked at in this way, you might image a tree growing outward from a vital center core, ring on ring through the seasons of its life. Looking at the cross section of the tree, you would see concentric circles, each circle as the tree looked to those around it in that season. That outer skin, those dimensions, must have seemed to the tree its very identity.

The tree is one of our oldest metaphors for the process of growth. In the Sumerian myth Inanna (about 2500 BCE) the goddess, as a young maid, tends the tree of life in her holy garden. "The years passed; five years, then ten years. The tree grew thick, but its bark did not split." Wild forces inhabit the tree: the snake "who cannot be charmed" lives in the roots; the wild maid Lilith in the trunk; and the anzu bird (lion/eagle) in the branches. The force of life grown large within her, Inanna cries out.[1] Something new *must* happen. When "the bark splits," new growth is happening.

 ### *Rings In The Tree of Life*

Draw your life as the cross section of a tree. Let each ring indicate your "identity" at that time. Who were you five years ago? Ten years ago? One year ago? Twenty years ago? Name or describe the rings. Trust the first thoughts, images, names that come to you.

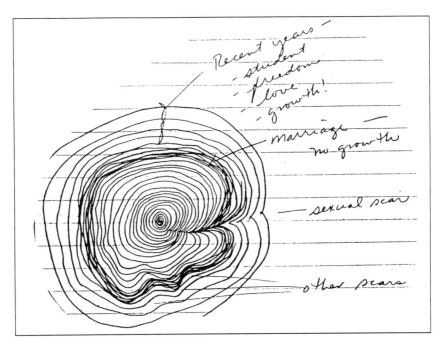

This journal sketch illustrates the way a scar might affect the tree of life.

 ## Seeing The Design

"I wanted to see how a scar would affect the rings of the tree," a woman told me after doing the last exercise, "so I put it in." "There is another thing I know about the way trees grow," she said. "When the conditions for growing are very good, they grow fast and have thick rings. When the conditions are difficult, they grow slowly and the rings are tighter together. That makes them tougher and stronger."

The exercise "Rings in the Tree of Life" allows you what might be called an "eagle's eye" view of your life. You are above and at a distance but able to zoom in for a close-up if you wish. This latitude — from the distance of the archetypal, to the closeness of the personal — is a quality of mythology as a language.

Look back at the image you created in exercise one but this time see it from a distance and see it as a design. Take a moment to simply see what it looks like. If you have the impulse to add to it or recreate it, go ahead. Sketch the design as a symbol of your growth.

 ## Photo Play

Select photographs of yourself at different times in your life (or use the photos in your mind). Create a collage by placing these images on the design of your growth you created in exercise one.

In your journal, give each a name that reflects who they are. For each, sketch what you would say if you were introducing this person as a character in a story.

Mirror, Mirror On The Wall

Mirrors are magical. Looking in a mirror is as close as we come to seeing ourselves "from the outside." At the same time, a mirror may give us the curious experience of seeing that we have more than one face. Sometimes there is even the shock of realizing that the face we see is not the one we imagined at all. Perhaps this is why many find it difficult to look at themselves.

To look into one's own eyes is to pass through many faces of the self, including some we may not like. In the film, "Neverending Story" one of the boy's initiations is to look into his own face. He is told many run screaming in terror when they must "face" themselves. In the world of fairy tale, the woman looking in the mirror on the wall, may not see the snow white beauty at all. In fact, she may see someone a lot more interesting.

Start by creating a safe space for yourself where you will not be interrupted. You may wish to alter the lighting, play music, put some of your favorite objects around you. Spend a few moments breathing and letting go of the tension in your body. Allow yourself to gaze at your face as you would meeting someone else, someone very familiar to you, someone you love and care about. Suspend judgement. Continue to gaze at your reflection, allowing the image to change and shift, allowing yourself to go more deeply. Take as long as you need to feel complete with the process. When you are ready, freewrite or draw what you remember of the experience. Who did you see?

 DANCE OF THE MASKS

In our earliest inscribed memories — Paleolithic cave drawings — people dance with masks: bird masks, animal masks, god or goddess masks. In Sumeria, Egypt, India, Africa, Turtle Island, everywhere, people have danced with masks. And when they danced, the spirit of the mask came — dancing bison, dancing eagle, dancing coyote. For a moment they became the other. They were themselves and something more.

Masks evoke an archetypal meaning; they allow us to go beyond ourselves — to see for a moment with the clarity of an eagle, or to recognize in the indigo field of stars painted across the mouth of our mask the opening to wisdom and truth being born in us. Because they are archetypal mirrors, masks both reflect us and evoke our growth.

In my apartment on a windy, December evening, the circle sat with their newly completed masks in front of them. "Let's dance with the mask," I said; "let's just move like the energy of our masks." We each took a simple instrument and began to play the song of our mask. Then we began moving, dancing our mask dance. Afterwards, when we sat quietly in the circle again, each of us knew something more about our archetypal selves.

There is a magic in mask making that is difficult to describe. Perhaps it begins with the surrendering necessary as you lie quietly, trusting the hands of another to move across the contours of your face, smoothing, shaping. You breathe, and let go of time as the mask begins to harden. Then comes the shedding, when snake-like you wiggle underneath this hardened skin, and slowly it is pulled from your face.

The first sight of one's face shell is almost always surprising. Do I look like that? Sometimes there is an immediate reaction to its appearance. I had a strong aversion to my first mask, so much like a death mask it looked. "You might as well just paint it gold," my circle friend, Gregory, said. I did. The newly created mask looked to me a lot like the Egyptian Scorpion Goddess, Serket, guardian of the gateway between death and rebirth. Scorpions, I read, carry not only the sting of death but the antidote to their own poison. Painting the mask gold was all I could handle the first week. The mask, however, has continued to evolve slowly over time.

Dwelling with the mask is an important part of the process. One woman placed her undecorated mask shell on the mantle over the fireplace in her living room. As she went through her week's routine, she passed by it frequently, being aware of it, but not thinking much about it. Then one morning as she walked through the living room, she stopped abruptly. Something about the mask told her that she was supposed to go back to the house where she had played as a child, even though it had long ago been sold to others. Following her impulse, making this journey back in time, she once more walked under the old maple trees and through the rooms of her childhood. When she came back, she knew how to create her mask.

 Mask Making

Although it can be done in a shorter time, an ideal circle process for mask making would be three two hour sessions. This leaves time in between for dwelling with the mask.

First Two Hour Session:

Supplies: You will need plaster coated gauze from a medical supply store, vaseline or other lubricant for the face, scissors to cut strips of gauze, a bowl of warm water, and towels.

1. Create a relaxed, safe environment. You might bring selections of favorite music to be played while you are being "masked." The person being masked should be lying comfortably with a towel wrapped around their hair.

2. Work in pairs. The mask maker works with an attitude of loving service. You are catching the imprint of this special face at this moment in time. Let your fingers communicate this attitude as you lubricate the person's face with vaseline. Remind them to breath and let go throughout the process. Dip gauze pieces in warm water and mold to their face, smoothing down edges with a little additional water. Apply several layers, leaving eyes (and, or course, nose holes!) uncovered.

3. Wait for about 30 minutes until the mask is hard. Music, stories, or guided meditations may fill the waiting time. When the mask is dry, have the person wiggle out with your assistance. Loosen the mask at the edges first. People are often in a very relaxed state. Let them take their time coming back. Have a bowl of warm water, soap, and towel ready for cleaning.

In between sessions: Place your mask shell, undecorated, somewhere in your private space and dwell with it. For some people the inside of the mask is as important as the outside and may be decorated in an entirely different way. Be aware of both the inside and the outside of your mask.

Second Two Hour Session:

Supplies: You will need paints, feathers, shells, yarn, materials, colored tissue, sparkleys — whatever else strikes the imagination.

You may wish to focus the mask decorating with music or with a journey of imagination such as "Unfolding Faces" or simply follow impulse in decorating. The decorating will probably continue after the session on into the week as people continue to dwell with their masks.

Third Two Hour Session:

Start with mask play such as wandering around the space in your masks, looking at each other, looking into mirrors, getting into the essence of the mask. Or do a Dance of the Masks.

When you are ready, come back into circle. Tell the story of your mask.

 Unfolding Faces

A Journey of Imagination: This journey may be used during mask drying when the person is relaxed and naturally aware of the skin like layer that is a mask of their face. Or it may be used to focus imagination and stimulate images before decorating masks.

Be sure you are in a safe and comfortable space. Become conscious of your breathing in and out, in and out.... Let your breath become like a silken stream, in and out.

Allow yourself to drift back in time, easily sliding back to the moment when your infant face was born into this world. For a moment see that tiny face, then feel its unfolding through the years — three years old, five, ten, sixteen — let the faces unfold through time until you feel yourself breaking through the surface of time, opening into this moment.

When you are ready, focus on your breath to bring you back into awareness of your body.

Sketch or name the faces that you saw.

 CREATING YOUR FRONT DOOR

The first class session of my college myth classes, I pose this question: If you were to place an image on your front door signifying who you are, what would it be? I ask people to create the image on the front page of their journal so that I may enter their journal through this doorway. They create these front doors in many ways, most often by drawing, painting, and collaging. Instinctively they know how such a symbol works, how it presents their essential beauty and strength to the world. Through this process, they create a "shield" or "coat of arms."

Over the last several millennia, these words have acquired connotations of war and aggression (as has the word "power" itself). One root of the word shield, "shild," meant quite simply to shelter. Like a house, a shield protects what is precious and vulnerable. I had been using the shell spider mandala (see page XII) as a door image of my work for some time before I realized that it was a shield. Although I knew it was described as a gorget, only recently did I realize that a gorget is a shield for the throat. Native women wore this shell mandala of Spider, the spinner, the creatress, over their throats. The throat was a sacred place, the source of sound, of story, of song. What a powerful reminder of their own creative expression, their own story telling, their own truth telling, it must have been.

Last summer in preparation for a family reunion, a relative sent me the Endicott family tree along with the family Coat of Arms. At first I was embarrassed and a little appalled by this ornate certificate. Certificate of Authenticity it proclaimed at the top of the document. It sounded straight out of the "Wizard of Oz," but what if some-one took it seriously? I grew up among farming folk in the Oregon countryside, and have a snobbish aversion to "class." I stashed it.

Then I began to wonder what this symbol meant to the people who had cherished it and passed it on as a "shield" of their family. I found the papers under the dresser in the "I don't know what to do with this file" and looked again at the shield. A grif-fin walks across the center on a path between three boldly drawn diamonds. That was it. Except for the words: "Argent on a fess azure between three fusils..." I had noticed that my "spell check" did not beep at "fusil." "Fire" the dictionary said.

My mind wandered on the images. I began to feel something I had never felt before: how deeply, how far back into my blood root, the aspiration of my family goes. In *Women Who Run With The Wolves*, Clarissa Pinkola Estes says that in earlier times, the word persona was "not simply a mask to hide behind." It was significator of character, of virtue, of authenticity, of outward mastery.[2] The shield had begun to seem to me like a statement of family persona. Still I preferred the older and friend-lier sounding Coat of Arms to shield.

A Coat of Arms. Through my arms, through my hands, I express and shape and do. A coat that signifies my pride in doing. Then I began to feel my arms as they have loved and held and nurtured — as they have opened the expression of my heart. At the same moment came the remembering of how they also protect me — hold away, draw the distance, throw, push, build, shape, establish boundaries. In these ways do my arms signify my power. I began to wonder: What Coat of Arms signifies me now?

Endicott family shield:
"Argent, on a fess azure, between three fusils gules a griffin passant or."

 Imagining Your Shield

1. If you were to place an image on your front door signifying who you are — what would it be?

2. If you were to place an image on the front door of your work, what would it be?

 Creating A Coat of Arms

1. Very quickly, without thinking about it too much, sketch your responses to each of the categories below. Sketching can be with words, images, colors, shapes.

ASPIRATION	STRENGTH (AUTHORITY)
INTEGRITY (VIRTUE)	SOURCE OF NURTURING
IDENTITY	WORK OF YOUR HANDS

2. Create your Coat of Arms. This may be a picture on the page or you may make it more tangible by using cloth, cardboard, or whatever your imagination suggests.

Exercises such as the last one often bring up shadows. This may at first seem odd, since the approach focuses on aspiration, on beauty. But that is just the point; it focuses on light. Shadows appear in the presence of light.

For instance, the mind can do something like this. My virtue: "honesty" (I'm not really honest. What about the time I had that secret affair. I am really a fake.) My aspiration: "to do the work of the goddess" (That's egotistical. My work is of no significance.) And so on and on.

I have come to think of these shadow thoughts and the feelings they evoke as "demons." I have a whole crew of them. But as I have gotten to know them better, I also recognize them more quickly. I picture them somewhat like the classic demon image in Buddhism: human in shape, but distorted — with a mouth like a pin point and a belly that is huge. They have an insatiable appetite, a need that cannot be satisfied, but almost no ability to open to the nurturing food of life. They immediately hear the negative and believe it. They cannot, however, open their mouth; they cannot be nourished. They cannot feel love: they cannot give love, they cannot receive love.

In the Sumerian myth, *Inanna*, the goddess Inanna's ear opens and she descends to "The Great Below." At each of the seven "gateways" she surrenders some of her powers until she stands naked and vulnerable before the wrathful eye of death. It is a stark portrayal of what Clarissa Estes calls "dying back to bones."

When, after three days and three nights, she is given the "bread of life" and "the water of life," she ascends from the great below followed by demons:

> *As Inanna ascended from the underworld,*
> *The galla, the demons of the underworld,*
>   *clung to her side*
> *The galla were demons who know no food*
>   *who know no drink*
>   *who eat no offerings*
>   *who accept no libations*
>   *who accept no gifts*
> *They enjoy no lovemaking.*
> *They have no sweet children to kiss.*
> *They tear the wife from the husband's arms*
> *They tear the child from the father's knees.*
> *They steal the bride from her marriage home.[3]*

When these demons from the Great Below ride around with us, we see and experience through their dark shrouds: we are unable to know the joy and pleasure of life. We are severed from those we love the most. At the same time, these demons are not extraneous to us. In a sense, they are the soul flagging us down, so we can see what needs to be healed.

In this way, demons are our teachers. They cling to us, nag us, haunt us, infuriate us, tempt us, take us by storm. They are a plague to our egos; they shatter and rip at our outworn personas. It takes courage, faith in the beauty of our essential self, to look our demons in the face for they do not reflect back our strength and beauty. Instead they feed on our weakness in the same way a virus or bacteria attacks the weak part of the body, the part in dis/ease. They continue to eat away at our vital self until they are recognized. They are similar to what Clarissa Estes calls "the predator;" they wait for the eye of confidence to blur. Then they go for that weak place.

These demons are not easy fellows to live with. That is their job: they test us. Barbara Walker points out that the word "demon," like so many words that describe the soul's journey, acquired its connotations of evil in the last couple of millennia. The word derives from the Greek daimon which meant a familiar spirit or guardian angel.[4] It is not so hard to see demon as a part of the self, but for most people it is a long way between the negative connotations of demon and the positive connotations of "guardian angel." For me, the bridge is to think of a demon as a difficult and exacting teacher.

 ## Shadow Play

1. Spotting the shadow
   Follow your first impulse in responding. Don't feel obligated to answer all.
   - What qualities do you most dislike in women? in men?
   - What contradictions came to you as you created your coat of arms?
   - How do you sit in judgement of yourself?
   - What are your self doubts?
   - What descriptions of yourself do you most dislike?

2. Go through your brainstorming, circling those words which evoke the strongest response. From these, choose the "demon" or "demons" you wish to work with.

3. Interaction with the demon:
   - Give them names (e.g. "The Red Wasp," "Opoorme," "Big Bertha"). Characterize them in drawing or writing, or dramatize them in action, costume, dialogue. Exaggerate the demons. Give them a typical expression or costume, a typical weapon.
   - What would your demons say about you if you left the room?
   - Ask them what they want. Invite them to a banquet — as in the Buddhist ritual, "Feast of the Hungry Ghosts" — and serve them whatever they want in abundance. Record the event in drawing or writing.
   - Have a conversation with your demon: what does it have to say to you? What do you have to say to it?
   - If you feel ready, choose a simple instrument and play a "swan song" for your demon. Change the demon into another form: re-draw, re-shape, re-write.

Who We Call Ourselves

Recently, I overheard a friend identifying herself by name over the phone and then spelling out her name in the common phone ritual of "A" as in apple, "D" as in dog. The description she gave of her name went "Z as in zoo and B as in boy." It made me chuckle because this strong, vibrant woman was certainly no "zoo boy." Then we started playing with what she might be: my favorite was "B as in beautiful, Z as in zealot." It seemed a name mirror that called forth her essence.

1. Free associate with the initials of your name until you find a name mirror that pleases you.

2. Write your name mirror in the center of a full page. Free associate around it. Write whatever comes up: images, emotions, contradictions, insights, names, memories.

3. Color or paint over the words using colors that are meaningful to you, for instance, orange for vitality, red for anger, grey for fear, green for growth. Notice patterns that emerge in the coloring.

4. Using color, design, images create a name shield that evokes the essence of your name mirror.

 ## Finding The Seed Stories

Using your name mirror, play with introducing yourself in a "story-like way." Playing around means just taking what pops into your mind, not trying. The description may be literal or imaginative, long or short. Playing around also means feeling free to break the rules if they don't feel right.

Story lines:

I am (gwendolyn) the (gifted) of (Wanderland Rainforest). I have come from the Land of (Self Small) and journey to (The Place of Listening).

I am the lioness, claudia
Of butterfly cave
I am from the mother's womb
I travel toward dharma...

From this initial playing around, you now have the seeds of four stories. I might title my stories:

1. "The Tale of gwendolyn, the Gifted" (persona)

2. "The Land of Wanderland" (place/present time)

3. "The Land of Self Small" (place — metaphoric, past time)

4. "The Journey to Listening" or simply, "The Journey to Ear" (metaphoric, present persona into future time)

Following Story Lines

1. Title your seed stories.

2. Notice if one of your titles stirs your feelings more than the others. See what story emerges. Letting the story emerge can be encouraged in several ways:

   Freewrite: When freewriting you let whatever comes to mind flow onto the page. You don't censor or judge. Keep writing without stop for at least ten minutes, even if your thought blocks. The motion of moving hand and pen helps loosen blocks.

   Question: Imagine you have met a stranger along the way who asks: "Who is gwendolyn, the gifted?" or "Where are you headed?" or "What is this place called Self Small like?" Create the dialogue.

   Free Associate: Write the title on a blank page. Let whatever pops into your mind or comes through your hand, flow out onto the page. Don't censor. Allow the possibility of shapes, images, pictures, as well as words.

 ## THE GIFTS OF NAME

A sacredness surrounds one's "true name." The traditions of many cultures have identified name with soul. In some of these cultures, one's soul name is so sacred that it is not spoken, or is only known by the few who are honored with the trust. In Egypt, the soul-name (the ren) "was breathed by a mother on her child as it was first put to her breast."[5] The Egyptian goddess of soul names was Renenet, the goddess who governed lactation.

Milk also poured in rivers from the breasts of the Great Mother. In Egypt, she is Hathor, wild cow of the heavens. From her breasts flow the "Milky Way." Many have believed that it is to this river of milky stars that souls return after death, still nurtured in the milk of the Mother. The oldest "baptism" was in the river of milk that flowed from the mother's breast, bestowing both naming and nurturing.

Prayer of gwendolyn, the gifted (formerly of Self-Small)

> *May I accept the gifts*
> *that are given to me*
> *in beauty*
> *may I accept and cherish*
> *the gifts that I am given.*

I am gifted with the beauty of Wanderland, Jeremy's face, these typing hands, the blue shifting moods of Luna's eyes, the sound of rushing waters....

Receiving The Gifts of Your Name

1. Who do you call yourself? (The answer may be the same as on page 11 or it may have changed.)

2. Dwell with the question: "What are the gifts of your name?" Answers may come in writing, sketching, collaging. You might try signing your name in the center of a page and then surrounding it with images of your gifts.

MOVEMENT 2

Mapping Your Pathways of Growth

All mythologies give us the same essential quest: You leave the world that you're in and go into a depth or into a distance or up to a height. There you come to what was missing in your consciousness in the world you formerly inhabited. Then comes the choice of either staying in that place with the gift you have received, or of bringing the gift back with you and trying to hold on to it as you move back into your social world again.

JOSEPH CAMPBELL, *The Power of Myth*

 ## MAPPING THE TERRITORY

"To chart the world, to make a map, was once a sacred art," I mused. It was a thought of little use to me in the moment. I was lost in Seattle, a city I did not know. Now keep in mind that I am an Oregon country kid who spends a lot of time in the rainforest.

"How do I get to…?" I asked the woman behind the counter of the service station. In Seattle "service" means *self* serve. She simply pointed to a map for $3.50. I realized she could not speak English. I sat in my car straining to read the tiny numbers and names that marked the maze of intersecting lines. Even with my glasses on, they blurred in and out of my vision.

One of my recurring nightmares as a child was trying to cross a city street. I remember my smallness in the expanse of street; I remember the buildings towering above me and the vertigo that swept through me, again and again. I had about thirty minutes to make it to my editing appointment with Waverly. "Plenty of time," I thought; "don't panic. You can figure it out." Finally, I asked a fellow customer, pumping his own gas, "Where am I on this map?" I took out a pen and charted my course through the maze of one small section of Seattle.

I had been re-reading and teaching Ursula Leguin's beautiful book, *Wizard of Earthsea,* and when I do, I live in the magical world of Earthsea. I love it there. On a double page preceding the story is the "Map of Earthsea." In the right hand corner of the map, the spirit of the winds, full cheeked, blows spiraling breath across the expanse of islands and seas, the archipelago of Earthsea. In the left hand corner, the journeyer steps forward, staff in hand. His foot almost touches the mandala of the four directions just ahead of him. It is created as both the traditional crossquarter of the directions (the earth's body) and as a zodiac wheel, the solar path. Ged, the journeyer of LeGuin's story, travels a path of initiation across land and sea to the "Farthest Reaches." The map of Earthsea is framed by a border of ten squares, each symbolizing an adventure, a mini-world that we enter through the doorways of the ten chapters in the book.

There was a time when drawing a map was a kind of magic; a cartographer "created" a world. With a map, others could "see" their world, from a distance, as if they had the eyes of a god, or an eagle. Even so, the map maker, acknowledging the limitations of human knowing, often placed an infinity sign in one corner of the map. This continuity of time was symbolized by two joined circles, an 8 on its side, or a snake eating its tail, the "Ouroboros." I love the feeling this gives of an expanse "beyond the map," and how my "world" becomes a circle within a circle within a circle... Some things, the symbol says to me, are "off the map."

"A map is never the territory," I thought. I had found my way to within about three blocks of Waverly's house when the street ended. I couldn't believe it. It had all looked so logical on the map. Driving "around the block" to find the street again turned into a maze of false possibilities. Huge, fallen trees from last week's storm appeared unexpectedly to block my passage. Finally I was on top of a hill, in a park, traveling around and around on a one way street. Totally confused, I drove into and out of this hill spiral several times. I was beginning to feel like I was back in that childhood nightmare, when suddenly Roosevelt Street reappeared. So did time. I was one hour late.

To this day, I don't know *how* I got there. And I certainly don't know how to get back again. In my map to Waverly's house there are many dead ends, many huge fallen trees and roots lying across the path, many people who point in the wrong direction, and a beautiful labyrinthian hill with fountains. I wonder — what will it look like when I travel there again?

 ### *Creating A Map of Three Lands*

Recalling your mythic "story lines" sketch the outlines of your three lands on one map. Follow impulse on size, shape, detail. Give the idea of "sketching" broad latitude. It may include color, shapes, words, buildings, weather, landscape, people, animals.

1. Draw the path of your journey through this landscape. Allow the possibility that the path may go down, up, in any direction.

2. Where are you on the path? What scenery is around you? What lies "up the path from you"?

Looking at the Boundaries:

Again sketch quickly whatever comes to mind. Let go of questions that don't work for you, rather than puzzling.

1. What lands surround you? Draw them in and name them. Who lives there?

2. Are there conflicts along the borders of the lands? Color them in or name them. What do the warriors of both sides look like? What weapons do they carry?

 Removing Boundaries

1. In your mind's eye, remove the boundaries between your three mythic lands.

2. Draw or create the shape of this new land. What is its name? Where are you in it? Put in the weather and major topographical features — buildings, gardens, wilderness, play areas, work areas. Is anything "off the map"?

 Journeyer

A Journey of Imagination:

Be sure you are in a comfortable and uninterrupted space. Begin conscious breathing: breathing in, filling your body with light; breathing out, releasing tension on the exhale; breathing in, breathing out.

See yourself walking along a path. Hear the sound of your footsteps as you walk. Notice where you are, what is around you, how the air feels against your skin. Notice how your body feels as you walk forward along this path.

Your excitement and curiosity about the land that lies ahead of you begins to grow and you quicken your pace. Then you notice a traveler approaching. You hear the sound of their footsteps as they come nearer and notice their appearance. You pause to speak to each other.

"What is it like in the land you come from?" the stranger asks. "Should I go there? Are there any dangers?" You answer as best you can.

"And what is it like in the land ahead?" you ask. And wait for a reply. Then you continue on your way, thinking about what has been said.

When you are ready breathe yourself back to present.

Record what you remember of the interaction and the advice given.

JOURNEY TO SELF SMALL

"The meaning of time is that, in it, stages of growth can unfold in clear sequence."[1]

When I first drew a map of my Three Lands, I noticed how rigidly I squared off The Land of Self Small — the area that I was "from." I drew the boundaries dark and definite. I knew by the quick, stark lines how sick I was of this place. I had lived here too long. I did not want to tell its story. But why had I named it then?

Another woman in the circle showed me her map; actually she was worried that it wasn't a map at all. "It came out in a spiral, all three in one," she said. She seemed a little disappointed as if somehow she had failed in the exercise. "I think you leaped right over the exercise," I said. "For you, there don't seem to be any boundaries to remove." I was struck by how spontaneously she had shed linear time. She, however, didn't seem quite comfortable with the fast spiral spin of all in one. I think she liked her boundaries a little tidier than this.

It is so easy to compare yourself to others when sitting in circle, and such a trap. For, of course, the experience, the lesson, and your personal mythology — all take place at exactly where you are. "How easily," I thought, "this woman sees her three worlds spinning together as one." Not so for me. I looked again at the boundaries. "Wanderland" and "The Land of Listening" easily became one, but I did not want to remove the walls that divided off "Self Small." I drew green lines, like sprouts pushing through into the present. That was the way I left it.

Not long after this circle session, I had a phone call. "You still haven't framed the house? How long do you think it is going to take you to build that place? Why don't you hire a contractor? The price of lumber is going up everyday. The summer is almost gone. That foundation is going to wash away. Do you even know how to drive a nail?" The voice went on. It was long distance and I was paying to listen to this teacher from Self Small. I was angry. For days I repeated the words to anyone who would listen, and defended myself. "I have worked since I was eight; I have supported myself since I was 18. I have raised three children. I am a competent person; successful in my profession, blah, blah, blah."

After several days of this, I began to realize how alive Self Small still was in me. I could hear the voice echoing far back into my childhood: "you can't do it; you have no ability; you will fail..." Then it was as if I turned. The focus changed. I heard the fear in the voice, instead of in me.

Sometimes in my sleep, I have what I call "experience dreams." They don't have the "distance" of usual dreams, no words, no plots. But something changes. When I wake up, I can still feel it. Something has happened. Not long ago, I dreamt that my heart opened to my father — there was simply a flood of love. When I awoke the next morning, it was still with me. I made the hundred mile journey to see him, in my home town, in the house where I lived as a teenager. We looked at old photo albums together, an 87 year old father, a 57 year old daughter.

I saw in the photos a love story. "I don't know why she ever married me," he said. I saw a young family in the depression years, the impact of war, of separation and fear. I saw family reunions and picnics, babies, aunts and uncles, and grandparents. I saw my dad in a sailor hat. Then we took a walk together, the two of us, on this cold February day, he in his lop-sided safari hat, the wind blowing harsh against his frail body, through a neighborhood I no longer knew.

Story is the plot we give to life, Theologian Thomas Berry reminds us. Story is woven from our basic assumptions and beliefs about how things work. A story sustains us, supports our emotional attitudes, and tells us who we are. Berry thinks that as a planet, as a culture, and as people we are in between stories. The old one doesn't fit anymore, but we have yet to spin the new one. I usually experience the place of "no clothes" (being in between persona) before realizing the story no longer works for me, but I think they are simultaneously happening. The story, after all, spins out from me, the story teller. As the walls of Self Small begin to crumble, I discover I am in the process of creating a new story. I am re-membering. I am stirring the birthing ground of my past, of my own down under; stirring and seeing, stirring and seeding.

 ## *Spinning The Yarn*

1. For several days observe the stories you are telling about yourself, your experience, the world around you. Don't try to change them; simply listen to them.

2. Make a list by title of the stories you hear yourself telling. For example, "Kicked Out in the Cold by a Mouse," "Coffee Snatcher," "Policemen are Lurking everywhere."

3. What are your favorite stories? Which do you choose to tell? List them by title or create a title page, a doorway into the story.

4. What stories that others tell about you do you choose to hear? Which are your favorites? Title them. Begin thinking of them as stories to be passed on to the future about you and your life.

 ## My Grandma's Forest

My favorite life story is also the only book that has ever been written about me. My grandson, Jeremy, wrote it when he was five years old. When I sent the early manuscripts of *The Spinning Wheel* to publishers, the story inspired some pointed remarks: "Including the story by your grandson is sheer self-indulgence," said one. "Maybe you should just publish this book for your family," said another. "We only publish Jungians," came a more lofty response. Overall, the message was clear: the stories of our children are of little significance.

Children begin to weave their personal mythology with their earliest words, naming what is significant to them. As language and awareness grow, they re-tell the stories that attract their attention and interpret the events of their lives with their own stories. If you wish to know the future that is growing around you, listen to the stories of the children. I would like to give you Jeremy's book the way it was given to me, in living crayon-color and bound in a Kinko's spiral, but I have had to make it conform to the page and the black and white of printer's ink.

I dedicate *My Grandma's Forest* to grandmothers everywhere who listen to the stories of the youngers, to my family and families everywhere, to my grandson, Jeremy, and to his children's children's children. May they know that their ancestor loved a rainforest and that it was magical.

My Grandma's Forest
by Jeremy

This is my dad and me having a party at my grandma's forest.

This is a tree with bark on it that is very old.

This is my gramdma's shroom.

*This is money lane
and brownies throw money.*

I am in my grandma's forest.

The end.

by Jeremy Wetter

MONEY LANE

As you can tell from Jeremy's story, "Money Lane" is an important mythic reality at Wanderland. This is the story of how it began in an impulse of play and how it continued in the delight of imagination.

• • •

"Do you put the money on money lane?" asked Jeremy. "What did you say?" I responded, slowing time to look for an answer.

It started in play and surprise for a five year old and had grown quickly into an important reality in Jeremy's mind. "Brownies spread the money at night for children under six to find," we told him the first time he came to visit Wanderland. And the Brownies had continued to drop coins under the alder along Money Lane every time Jeremy came, past the year of six into seven, until now he stood before me, and there was no avoiding the question: "Do you put the money on money lane?" he repeated.

"Sometimes. Sometimes I get a Brownie urge and let fly with the coins, " I replied.

No surprise. He knew it. Only did not want to lose the magic (or the money). "What do you think Brownies look like?" he asked.

Jeremy is very honest. And you had better be too, or you lose his interest immediately.

"Well, I think they are very close to the earth and not easy to see. Much that is real we cannot explain with our minds. I think Brownies are a way we have of describing the magical and mysterious ways of earth."

"The Brownie I know best is Jack Frost," replied Jeremy. He comes between night and dawn. You can try trapping him. He has a white beard and paints the earth white. He carries a sack on his back with squirt guns and candy in it."

My mind was racing trying to keep up with him. "Why squirt guns and candy?" I asked.

"Because he plays tricks," said Jeremy.

That night at Wanderland, Jeremy made a trap with a cardboard box, chocolate chips, and quarters.

 Listening To The Children

Listen to the stories of the children around you. What are their favorite subjects? Give their stories titles. What do these stories reveal about the way the children see their world?

 FOLLOWING IMPULSE

"Then, he went right on his way again... making those tracks, tracks, tracks..." says story teller Susan Strauss. That old man coyote, following his nose, following his curiosity, letting his impulse lead him into adventure — and mishap. But he is almost impossible to kill. Like Road Runner, he picks himself right up again, making "tracks, tracks, tracks..." into more experience.

Often he is the fool — caught "dead in his tracks" trying something new somewhere he shouldn't be or off sleeping or eating, dancing or just tracking, when he should be home taking care of his responsibility.

Coyote is creative fire, sexual desire; coyote is that impulse, that curiosity that pulls us toward the new. Coyote teaches us through experience, through sometimes falling flat on our face.

COYOTE SONG

Once a woman sang out to coyote, "Come dance with me, Coyote Woman, come dance with me!" She sang and sang to the fire, "O Coyote come dance, come dance!" In her vision Coyote came. She heard coyote feet, saw coyote eyes, glimpsed coyote smile in the moonlight. "Follow me," Coyote said. "Follow me."

She ran fast along the trail, feeling the heat of coyote breath. Faster and faster they ran into the night. She let go as she ran, let go as she ran, until finally she let her body go, too, falling to the ground under the star lit night. Alone in a clearing she sat listening, naked and alone. She heard Coyote howling. She heard coyote laugh. "I will take everything, everything!" Coyote sang.

 Coyote Tracks

1. List times that following impulse has gotten you in trouble. Title these stories.

2. List times that following impulse has led you to new discovery. Titles.

3. List times you have "fallen flat on your face." Titles.

4. Choose one of your titles and write a coyote teaching story for the "youngers" of your tribe.

 ## CROSS ROADS

At cross roads a choice is made. To stand at the center, at the intersection of crossroads is to stand in the midst of possibilities. It is the center of the cross, the hub of the wheel. From this place, purpose or goal is focused, and, at the same time, possibilities are narrowed. Some roads are possible, but not chosen. At crossroads, one thing is pruned in order for another to grow.

The dark moon goddess, Hecate, who has the wisdom of age, is associated with crossroads, for they are both an ending and a new beginning as the dark moon is the seed from which the new grows. In the Mother Peace tarot deck, "The Crone" is Hecate at the crossroads, hand cupped to her ear, listening to the voice of inner knowing. When the old way ends and a new way is to unfold, when we stand in the midst of possibilities, choice is best guided by our deepest desire.

Standing At The Cross Roads

If you are presently "standing at a cross road," knowing you must make a choice, try looking at the situation from a distance by mapping it. Draw the path choices as lines intersecting. The point of intersection is where you stand, in the midst of all the, as yet, undeveloped possibilities. Label the paths; for each, put in the possibilities with words or images.

Following impulse, color in your feelings around each path. Dwell with the overall pattern of this cross road. Which paths most attract you?

 Sign Posts

Looking back at the path you drew through your three lands, put in the cross roads. Where did you choose to go one way rather than another? Create signs to mark your major cross roads. Put the possibilities you let go of on the map as names of unvisited places. Where did you choose to go instead?

 Heart Line

Draw a heart line, or perhaps you prefer a heart "vine," through your three lands. Where has your heart opened? Where has it closed? Where has it been pruned?

 PORTALS ARE THRESHOLDS TO A NEW REALITY

A portal, or gateway, is the threshold that marks the changing of our reality. In Sumerian mythology, the river god Enki, with his two faced servant Isimud, is guardian of gateways. Impulsive, and, at the same time, called God of Wisdom, Enki is as changeable as the river or the tides of emotion. He symbolizes the initiations that come from the wisdom of time and experience — what we know now that we didn't know before. Because of this, he is a two-faced god: looking back and looking forward; looking out from himself and looking into himself. His emblem is a vessel with two rivers flowing in and out.

Initiations are like portals: we pass through into a new reality, a new landscape. We know we are passing through when the place we have been seems like a distant land. "Visualize a gateway on a hilltop," says the Rune "Thurisaz" (Gateway). "Your entire life lies behind you and below. Before you pass through, pause and review the past: the learning and the joys, the tests and tribulations, all that it took to bring you here. Bless it and release it all."[2] In this way, you make yourself ready to walk on.

Portals of Initiation

1. Sketch quickly or name the portals of initiation you have passed through.

2. Decorate your portals to symbolize the essence of the initiation you passed through.

3. Sometimes there are "gate keepers"; those who hold the secret to passage. Who was the gate keeper? What was the key? Was there a lesson or teaching received?

4. Sketch the landscape on both sides of the portal.

5. Sketch the persona you were before passing through and after.

Enki, Sumerian god of doorways and initiation, is described as
the God of Wisdom. (2330 BCE)

 Gate Keeper

A Journey of Imagination

Be certain you are in a safe and uninterrupted space. Focus on your breath: breathing in, filling with light; exhaling, releasing the tension from your body. Breathing in and out until you feel relaxed and grounded.

See yourself walking along your path; you will know where you are. Become aware of the scenery that surrounds you, the sound of your feet on the path. You are not in a hurry, but as you walk, you feel the path grow steeper and your body strains a little as you climb slowly upward.

In the distance, the top of the hill begins to take shape in your vision. At the same time, you see the outline of a gateway, growing larger as you climb. As you approach, you pause to rest and to contemplate this place, listening to the sound of the water cascading in a waterfall nearby. You see the land below you, in the distance, and give thanks for where you have been. Then you refresh yourself, splashing the water over your hands and face.

Ahead of you is the gateway, the passage to a new place. You wonder what lies beyond. You wonder if it is time to pass through. You know there is a keeper of this gate; one who knows both sides and wishes you safe journey. You ask very simply, "May I pass through?" You wait for the answer and are willing to hear.

In the opening of the gateway, you feel the gate keeper very near and you know that, if you ask, you will receive a tool — a talisman or perhaps a compass — to guide you as you continue your journey in this new land. Give yourself as much time as you need for this interaction.

When you are ready, use your breath to guide you back into the present.

Record what you remember of this experience.

 ## Archetypal Portals

1. Create a portal to the Garden of Paradise.

2. Create the portal to a Holy Place.

 ## Elemental Portals

One of my favorite images is of the Sumerian sun god, Shamash, rising between two mountains at the horizon (Akkadian seal, 3rd Millenium BCE). Rays of creative energy emanate from his body; two lions guard the Eastern gates of the horizon. As he rises between the mountains at the Eastern portal, one imagines the robes of night flowing behind him, the glow of dawn flowing before him. He steps forward into the new day.

The dance of sun, moon, and earth teach us of elemental portals. In circle, a young man spoke of how his portals were the doorways of the seasons; his own inner processes so closely followed their cycles of birth and death and rebirth.

Play around with creating elemental portals. Let impulse determine which ones.

EAST	SOUTH	WEST	NORTH
SPRING	SUMMER	FALL	WINTER
SOURCE OF THE WATERS	SOURCE OF FIRE	SOURCE OF WINDS	
SUN RISE	SUN SET		
MOON RISE	MOON SET		
PORTAL OF THE MOUNTAIN			

Shamash Akkadian seal,
3rd millenia BCE

RIVER OF LIFE

For one as rooted to place as I am, the metaphor of life as a journey along a "path" comes quite naturally. Perhaps it is my Capricornian nature; I love the feel of the earth under my feet. Perhaps it is the generations of my ancestors who loved this place before me. Forests and rivers and oceans. Mountains and valleys and orchards. Rains, mists, rainbows and sometimes snow. Winds and storms and the smell of the earth dying back to itself in fall as alder leaves rot into the forest floor. With the first warm day of early spring, the earth opens in new green and the smell in the air of the warming earth and the opening plants makes you feel like you are in heaven. How could I want to be anywhere else. Waverly tells me, "There are a lot of trees in this book." "I live in a rainforest," I answer. The images of our mythologies arise out of our experience.

On the evening of the Winter Solstice, I asked my son, Michael, to tell a story. Michael's Winter Solstice stories have become a tradition we look forward to at this gathering. He does not seem to plan them; they grow as he speaks, episode by episode from some deep place in himself. Last year's story was about a village that had forgotten how to celebrate cycles and turn the wheel of change, and of a small boy who remembered by journeying deep into the earth. This year Michael told a story of The River of Life, how in its currents, people and events are swept from his outstretched hands as his boat moves rapidly downstream. "Last year it was a path; this year a river," I said. "Really?" he replied.

Michael is a walker; he hiked the Pacific Crest Trail when he was 20. It took him six months, step by step from the border of Mexico to the border of Canada. I love the pictures I have of him on this trip. He is tall and young and beautiful. In one, he sits beside a clear mountain pool carved from stone; wearing his best, black pants and white shirt while he plays his flute to the mountain. I do not think Michael could choose, however, between mountain and river — especially the kayaking, where body and boat are one in the currents. Since Jeremy's birth, eight years ago, however, rafting has become the new river play.

Winter Solstice usually sends Michael deeply into himself in a dying back that is, by now, familiar to him. It is the time of his birth, and it is the time when his personal cycle merges with the seasonal cycle. Some years he simply comes in, stretches out full length on the floor amidst the people, all 6 foot 4 and 200 pounds of him, and goes under. He hears nothing. The evening is filled with drumming, dancing, story telling, talking — all around and over Michael. He hears nothing. In the silence of early morning, he comes back to waking consciousness, and rises as if shaking an outworn skin from his powerful body. This solstice night, he had just returned from a two day retreat celebrating his thirty-third birthday. In the telling of his Solstice story, I felt how fast and deep the river was running for him.

"I just got a river image from the tarot," I told him. "An eddy" — what do you think that means?" "An eddy is a current of whirling water flowing in the opposite direction from the main current," Michael explained. "You get caught by it and spin around and around until it spits you out again," It was a perfect metaphor for what I was experiencing — going around and around, caught in the same familiar patterns and emotions. It also gave me a sense of why it was so difficult to get out of this place.

In Greco-Roman mythology there is a great river flowing around the rim of the earth. Sometimes this river is imaged as a serpent with its tail in its mouth, symbolizing the continuousness of time. The name of this serpent was "Oceanus," which Barbara Walker says meant "He who belongs to the Swift Queen."[3] Oceanus is the stream of time itself, but also controls the changes in the world, the cycles. This, says Marie-Louise von Franz, is the mystical "round element" (Omega) that symbolized "a life time," "a period of time," and "an eternity." Time, as a river, is experienced as a constant flow of inner and outer events.

von Franz believes all river gods were male and often associated with the horns of the bull because they represent dynamic forces. The river god "wells up from Elysium, the timeless land of bliss."[4] There is a danger in thinking that "dynamic forces" belong only to the male. There is, for instance, an absolutely beautiful image of the river goddess, Yamuna Devi, standing in a sea portal of tortoises and crocodiles.[5] Goddess of the river Juma, in India, she is the source of the waters of life. Her portal is the gateway to the "timeless land of bliss." How does one separate the source from the stream?

In Sumerian myth, Enki is a river god, associated with the fertilizing powers. The Sumerians connected the river of life with the male; water and semen in Sumerian are the same word. The Sumerians lived on the land now called Iraq between two great rivers, the Tigris and the Euphrates, that flowed into the ocean. Yearly, the rains would come, the rivers would swell, the land would be fertilized in the rising and falling of the waters. Enki's throne described as "directly above the underworld," is where the rivers meet with the ocean.[6] Enki's emblem is a vessel with two rivers flowing in, flowing out. In their mythology, the Sumerians saw the fertilizing river of life, flowing from the source and back to the source, as sacred.

 River of Life/Sketching

On a long sheet of newsprint or black roofing paper, sketch your life as a river. Where did it spring from the earth? Where are the rapids, the deep pools, the stagnate marshes, the eddys, the waterfalls, the forks...

 TREE OF LIFE

It is probably safe to guess, that the tree of life appears as a mythic image everywhere on the earth that people have lived with trees. Some mythologies, such as the Sumerian, tell of how the tree is born of the rushing rivers and torn by the South Winds. The goddess Inanna plucks it from the river and plants it in "her holy garden," tending it as it grows. The tree swells with wild, untamed life force, reflecting the growth and maturation of the goddess/woman in the myth. The snake, who "cannot be charmed" is curled at the roots ready to rise. It is an old, old image, an image that comes from ancient goddess cultures — this image of goddess as the growing changing force of life; this image of goddess as tree, with the snake of creative force rising within her.

Our mythic roots show that people saw the spine of our bodies as a tree of life. The serpent fire, Kundalini, rises up the trunk, branching and blossoming in the wheels of light some call chakras. Snake takes wings in spirit flight from the branches of the tree. Medical professions still use this stylized tree as a symbol — two snakes climbing a central pole, with bird wings at the top.

Marija Gimbutas' research shows us there is a good reason to believe that disectionists from these old cultures saw a similarity between woman's reproductive system and the tree.[7] The tree of life was within woman and was pulled in its growing and dying by the cycles of the moon. A wonderful painting by contemporary artist, Meinrad Craighead, show a woman tree growing in the center of a garden, fallopian tube branch/arms fruiting eggs from her mysterious and abundant center.[8]

The tree connects us to the source and to the cycles of time and change as does the image of the river of life. It represents past, present, and future; it represents generations of growth, as in a family tree; and it represents our own personal maturation, blossoming, dying. The tree also shows us how we live in all three worlds simultaneously as states of consciousness: the underworld (of death and rebirth); this world (of experience and change); and the upperworld (of spirit flight).

 ## Tree of Life/Sketching

Draw or collage a tree of life. Let its roots be what "feeds" you from the past, what gives you strength, balance, nurturance.

Give the trunk the shape and appearance of how you are growing in the present.

Let the branches show how you are "reaching out"; how you are branching out into the new. In their reaching, put your desires, your hopes, your dreams, your visions.

Let its blossoms be the "eggs of possibility," what is opening for you to choose from.

And in its fruit put what has come, is coming to completeness in your life. Some may also be releasing, falling back into the earth.

Color the snake of sexual energy up the tree — showing how it changes and moves, closes and opens.

What animals live in and around the tree?

In the breezes, in the flight of birds, in the glow from sun, moon, and stars, put your songs of thank-fullness.

 ## Close Up

Let impulse guide you to a part of the tree of life you have just created. Go into this part by doing a "close up" of it on a separate page.

MOVEMENT 3

Finding The Center Place

Spiraling into the center, the center of the shield
Spiraling into the center, the center of the shield
I am the weaver, I am the woven one
I am the dreamer, I am the dream
I am the weaver, I am the woven one
I am the dreamer, I am the dream

> from "Spiraling Into the Center" a song by Lorna Kohler
> 1988 Acoustic Medicine Productions

 ## GOING HOME

Finding a special book is for me like meeting a special person. The memory of that first meeting begins the myth of the relationship. Around six years ago, I returned to my home town to be with my father during surgery. The crisis over and my father sleeping, I escaped the hospital to wander nearby bookstores on the university campus. My mind had posed a request: let me find a new book for my Images of Women class. I walked through aisles and aisles of books in several large bookstores; many of the books were interesting, but none quite right. On my way back to the hospital, I saw a small shop with books specially displayed among the crystals in the window. "When I was in college, that was the corner drugstore," I thought. It looked quiet and inviting.

On the shelves of this small shop, I first saw *The Mother's Songs* by Meinrad Craighead. I had that excited feeling of holding a book in my hands I could hardly wait to read. That night, time disappeared as I disappeared into the book, merging with Craighead's images. I read the whole book, cover to cover. And passed out.

I tell people: "Do not try to read Meinrad Craighead's work; dwell with it, page by page. Slowly." Craighead's paintings and her words have the quality of dream (many *are* dreams) and like dream, they continue to unfold within you, layer after layer, through the days, and months, and years. People who love books know the feeling of finding one that is "right"— how it rushes in and fills you. This is the relationship I have with Craighead's books. And this is why I do not know if this dream I am going to tell came before the reading of *The Mother's Songs* or after. But I know the dream. Craighead calls it "Journey;" I call it "Going Home."

For Craighead the dream comes repeatedly, only her point of departure each time is different. She is leaving a large city journeying through ever smaller cities and remote villages, and then across an endless landscape of earth and sky. She abandons her car and starts walking, carrying a small white puppy. She travels for days across the vast continent of her dreamscape until she reaches the sea. At the edge of the sea grows a great pine tree. She walks into the darkness, into the substance of the tree, circling "through the multiple, concentric rings of the tree, shrinking and aging within each ring." When, at last, the spiraling ends, she has arrived "at the small dark spot of origination." "When I touch this innermost center," she says, "I realize I am already there. I have been journeying to where I am."[1]

My own dream came in two parts. In the first dream, I travel from a strange city through ever smaller villages into the countryside, not knowing where I am, but sure that I am headed toward home. I am getting closer and closer. I can feel the excitement, the yearning in my belly. The dream ends, however, before I can reach my destination. Several months later, I awoke with an in-body dream experience. "I'm home" were the words that followed me into consciousness. I could still feel the "rushing in," but the house was my body. I didn't know how to explain it to people. Although the experience of the dream grew dimmer over time, in some way I had come back home in myself.

When I was going to college in the fifties, Thomas Wolfe's novel, *You Can't Go Home Again,* was popular among sophisticated college students. We drank coffee or beer and talked about despair; we read Sartre, Eliot, Dostoevsky, and Crane. The attitude of separation and cynicism followed me through the years and still prevails on college campuses where I teach. And so, it is with some surprise that I not only discover that I *can* go home again, but that "home" is exactly where I must go.

The word "home" also has verb forms — "homing" and "homed." People once spoke of a "homing instinct;" now we tend to speak of it in missiles rather than ourselves. They are guided, homing toward their targets. Even this use however, says that homing is part of "the system," that it is automatic, instinctual, guided. Spiraling into the center, we know the way back home.

 ## Homing

1. Where does your homing instinct pull you?

2. Draw a map of your personal living space. Color in areas where you feel most "at home." Notice where and how much of the space you are at home in. How far into surrounding areas (neighborhood, city…) do you feel at home?

3. What are you most at home doing?

LOSING TRACK OF TIME

Time, according to folk-wisdom, goes faster as you age. I heard this concept repeated again recently, along with the remark that this is because the old move more slowly. For a moment, I almost accepted this powerful thought form about aging without question. Then I realized that I no longer knew if "my time" was moving fast or slow. I had lost most of my markers in time.

When I was a child, I worked beside my grandfather weeding and hoeing fields of sorghum and picking peaches in the orchards. We had conversations about God and time. Sometimes, "to pass the time," we played a game, guessing the hour by the sun and the feel of earth and air. I became very good at knowing time intuitively and rarely have worn a watch.

The schedules of being a student and then teaching put me on linear time: there were Monday, Wednesday, Friday type days and Tuesday, Thursday days. And there was summer vacation. Now, as I write and teach and work at Wanderland on my own time, I have trouble remembering what day it is. In the dentist's office last week, the friendly assistant asked me, "Did you have a good weekend?" I tried to focus fast enough not to show that I didn't have a clue we had passed a weekend. I had been working at Wanderland. Not to mention, of course, that "weekends" have no relevance to me anymore. I realized how far out of time I had become, however, when I had to stop, sit down, and figure out my age. Fifty-eight it added up to. Quite remarkable. I felt, for a moment, like the ancient mother in one of Kurt Vonnegut's novels who rasps out "How did I get this old?!"

A year ago, a friend gave me the page of her calendar that was the date of my birth. On it were two quotations. The first was a line from Meridel Le Sueur: "Lying, walking, sitting in this room, she felt herself ripening and coloring." The other was the calendar thought for the day: "Remember! I could not know what I know today if I weren't the age I am. I have the continued opportunity to grow." Her gift of the calendar page stays on my altar so that I can remind myself when I forget.

Those who are no longer in linear time have an opportunity to experience living more in "dream time": in memory, imagination, dream, and vision. Frequently, I think it is not that "old people move more slowly" but that they move on a different track. This is a gift of time.

Supposedly I have "retired." People ask me "How is retirement?" It always surprises me. I have never had more work of the hands. Nor have I ever done more work of the mind or ventured into more creative projects. Still, my relationship with time *has* changed. When I begin to feel overwhelmed by work, by what needs to be done, I don't race with time, I surrender to time. I do this with an asking prayer: "May there be the time for what needs to happen, to happen, for what needs to unfold to unfold. May the work be done successfully." Then I let go and take time moment by moment.

Inhabiting Time

1. On a large sheet of paper, draw a shape that represents "your time."

2. Who/what "occupies" your time? Create size by amount of time; texture, shape, color might be the feeling you have about that time. Change outer boundaries as you like.

3. In your drawing, create the "outer space" by drawing or coloring in what would like to come into your "circle" of time.

4. Look at the boundaries between "time zones." What is the weather like there? (e.g. stormy, electric, windy, turbulent, foggy, hurricanes, tranquil). Draw or write a landscape of this border. Where is it rough, mountainous, boggy, watery? Are there bridges across the boundaries?

5. Are there any animal or plant teachers in your time map? Draw them in spontaneously without question or analysis. What are their gifts?

6. Notice if there is conflict *between* boundaries. What are the issues? Where does the conflict take place? What are the weapons? Do you favor one side or the other? Sketch or freewrite how you see the side you favor least. Give the story of the war between time zones a title. Create a dialogue between the major characters of the zones. ("Trying," the person who wants to get it *all* done; "Alone," the person wanting to write a book; "Bliss," the person who wants to just put it all down and en-joy.)

WHOSE TIME IS IT? (A LOVER'S DILEMMA)

You tell me: You resent that I have taken over your time. I occupy your mind. Your life was just fine before I came along. So simple and all yours. You don't want to need me in your space, but where have I been and what have I been doing with my time? You tell me your schedule, your commitments; you tell me how busy you are. You have no time.

I tell you: I had fully occupied my time when you came along. My life was spinning just fine. I felt alive and creative and full of myself. Why would I want to give you my time? No. I intend to sit full in the middle of it all. I will fill it with my self.

But maybe, on a whim (not a time), might we share joy, or adventure, or pleasure, or love?

 *Time Talk*

1. Have a conversation with "your time." Tell it where it pleases you; where it doesn't; where you have problems with it; how you wish it would change. Talk about the "power struggle" between you. Who is in charge of the relationship — you or time?

2. Create a dialogue with someone close to you about your relationship with time.

 ## THE SECRET SONG

I think I was about five years old when I discovered song. I remember singing in the sunlight of my bedroom, singing in the garden among the flowers, singing whenever I was alone. I sang about the sunlight and the birds and the ladybugs, about whatever was around me. I had no doubt that my voice and my song were incredibly beautiful. My song, however, was a secret. No one knew about it but me. In fact, this is the first time I have told of it.

By the time I was ten, my world and my family had been fractured by the second world war. I had no bridges to the adult world and no clue how to communicate with other children. A great loneliness was around me. I remember one summer picking beans, singing and singing, thinking perhaps I would be "discovered" by the older girl in the next row whom I admired. This did, indeed, happen. How could she help but hear me? She called me over. "Sing for me," she said. I didn't know how.

When I was in the sixth grade, I discovered that I could not sing. I remember standing miserably in front of the class singing "O Little Town of Bethlehem" in a screeching, halting voice. And then came the violin. You could rent them for six dollars a month and be in the school orchestra. We went on tours to other schools. I am not sure where I was supposed to learn how to read music, but I didn't. I had no idea how the symbols on the paper, the sound, and the strings corresponded. I watched the person next to me to see what string to play. Finally, I gave up. I believed that I had no song.

The child who sang in the beauty of the moment I call the "essential child." She lives in a place of innocence where she is simply at home in herself, close to the pulse of her being. Most people can still remember that place in themselves, and are reminded of it by the faces of children. When Jeremy was small, I used to love taking him to ride the antique merry-go-round in downtown Portland. As the merry-go-round picked up speed, Jeremy would go galloping by on his favorite horse, Popcorn, head thrown back in joyous laughter, his round face, his whole two year old body alive in the total bliss of that moment. I remember how the people would gather with me to watch the joyous Jeremy ride and laugh with him.

In the Tarot the child is "O," The Fool. We return to this place of newness again and again in our journey. Ever changing and yet always the same, it is a place without masks where we are close to source. Within us, it is the seed self. In the imagery of universal beginnings, the Chinese have called this center the "Pearl of

Beginning, the germ of the universe."[2]

The Pearl of Beginning within you is the seed essence from which you grow. One way of touching back to that essence is by remembering the "essential child;" this is not the fractured or injured child, but rather that place within where you still remember being totally alive in a timeless moment.

 ## *Remembering The Essential Child*

A Journey of Imagination

Be sure you are in a safe and comfortable place. Breathe deeply, feeling the inhale filling your body, the exhale releasing tension. Continue to breathe in this conscious way until you feel relaxed and present in yourself.

Allow your mind to drift back, back through the years to a time when you played happily as a child. See yourself playing, totally absorbed in what you are doing, oblivious of time, conscious only of your play, following your impulse, your curiosity, exploring, experiencing. Where are you? What are you doing? Allow yourself to remember what it felt like to your senses — perhaps the feel of the sun on your skin, the smell of pansies in the air, the blue of the sky, the wind in your hair. Take as long as you like to remember this moment.

When you are ready to come back to present, focus again on your breath. As you become more focused in present, look back for a moment more at the child at play. See how beautiful this child is. Remember the child's pleasure.

Describe the child experience in words, colors, or images.

 ## *Dwelling Place*

For a few days or more, notice where you are "dwelling." Where do you pause and simply allow yourself to be. Be particularly aware of the times when you "should be doing something else" and you find yourself dwelling.

Name these places or give them form in writing or sketching. These are your "dwelling places."

 ## BECOMING HOUSEMATES WITH EARTH

I have a garden at Wanderland. Some think it strange that I have a garden before a house. I have had a garden for two years already; the house grows much more slowly. I call the garden "Spike Garden" because I created it from a pile of old tree bones that had been thrown among the fern and foxglove near the old logging turn-around that is now the Wander House site. Spike Garden grew from silvered roots, hardened tree cores, and knots weathered into fantastic shapes.

Quite simply, to make a garden gave me comfort; it eased the abruptness of moving from a 2,000 square foot, suburban home to a 9 by 10 shed in the rainforest.

I confess, that first afternoon when the idea of a garden came to me, I felt a little like Edward Scissorhands — my hands flew so quickly into the shaping. Paths wound around wood sculptures and fern and foxglove. I brought in stones and sand and new plants and wind chimes. Frog and turtle, snake, salamander, and slug were totemic in the garden. Bees, butterflies, and hummingbirds make frequent visits.

It is easy to feel possessive of a space. After a year of planting and tending, I began to feel at home: it was *my* garden. I had a habit of sitting in the hollow between the roots of an old cedar stump in the garden. It was a wonderfully comfortable chair — a soft seat of mossy earth, moss covered arms, a tall cedar back. I would sit there in the early morning, sipping my coffee, or listening to the forest, or in meditation, humming.

This simple 9'x 10' shed, built by hand the first winter at Wanderland,
is fondly called "the shroom"— one room in a rainforest.

It was there I sat one summer afternoon this year, full only of sun and sound, when I was startled by a vocal tone —"ahhhh"— coming from directly in front of me. Hovering before my face was a huge golden bee. For a second longer, I heard the human tone vibrating before it became bee hum. Then the bee circled slowly over and around me and disappeared between me and the stump. I jumped up shaking my clothes. I wanted no bee down my back. But she was gone.

A few weeks later as I sat in my garden throne, I was again startled aware — this time by a loud buzzing. "What are those? flies buzzing around me?" I thought, still sitting motionless. Just then, one dived and stung my hand. I was out of the stump in a flash.

And so I was abruptly thrown out of my garden that day. It was clear that the queen had entered and occupied her space. Her warriors thought this obvious and me not only stupid but quite simply in the way. She was primary; I secondary to this place.

There are some who do not understand this story. They tell me ways of burning or poisoning bees. And I tell them of the black mud wasps that lived in a mound right across from the shed. "We have to burn them out," we thought. Three times we set fire to the nest; three times we watched the survivors carry away the dead and rebuild their home before we realized that these bees were not bothering us, not once had we been stung. They were just living there. Now we go around their nests if we can, and they rarely build in our paths.

"Walk gently, listen to the earth," says the sign I painted and hung at the entry to a path into the forest. It is there to remind me. The full quote is "Walk gently, listen to the breathing underneath the feet." It comes from one of my favorite sections of Evelyn Eaton's book, *Snowy Earth Comes Gliding*. Indian ecology, says Eaton, "is based on the belief that everything created by the Great Holy is equally important and has its rightful place; that there is an interdependence of created things."[3]

I do not wish to give the impression that this is an easy attitude to cultivate or that I have mastered it. I remember the day I opened the shed door to see ants four columns deep, marching up all the corners to the ceiling and across the ceiling. I had, just the day before, moved into the shed. It was my only shelter in the forest. I drove to town, bought a can of Raid, emptied my belongings from the shed onto the road, and bombed it. The next day as I swept up what seemed like thousands of black ant bodies, I mused about mythological ants. I thought they were supposed to *help* with the task like they do in the tale of *Cupid and Psyche*. These ants of mine kept me sorting and resorting my belongings for yet another day. Since then, I have learned that a little "Buzz Off" with citronella, on the door-sill keeps the ants out.

I wonder sometimes if our human mobility, our rootlessness of mind and body, makes us obsessed not only with occupying but with controlling and owning space. Trees and plants are rooted to place; animals and birds have their niche, their habitat. They know when they are "home." Humans, however, have a very bad reputation in this matter, especially in the last five thousand years.

So natural does human priority seem to most, so ingrained in ways of seeing and acting, that it begins to make perfect sense that *our* laws determine what happens to *our* "natural resources." Last year I stood listening to a nice young man from the State Forestry Department while he explained to me (as if I were a bit out of line for asking) that the Forest Practices Act of the state of Oregon specifies that a state owned forest (even if it *is* a watershed) may be clear-cut within 50 feet of my spring, "leaving two trees and two logs per acre for the wildlife."

Sometimes, in my mind's eye, I see those two trees and those two logs, like an island amidst the clear-cut, teeming with all the creatures of the forest. Is it some mad mythological descendent of the Noah's Ark legend that we see our forests vanish leaving only two trees to seed again the scorched earth?

Once I dreamt that huge fallen tree bodies lay upon a darkened earth. In the dream, I heard the voice of the trees speaking to each other. "They are coming! They are coming! The people are coming!" It was the voice of hope not fear. Then, as clear as mid-day reality, I was walking down a sunlit forest path; the forest was singing, filled with wild-life and with birds. "We are recreating, I thought, as I floated into consciousness. "The earth knows we are recreating."

Housemates

1. Joseph Campbell points out that if we changed our habit of using the pronoun "it" in referring to animals and used, instead, "thou," our whole way of seeing animals and interacting with them would change. Practice this shift for several days. Record what you experience.

2. What places on the earth do you consider special or sacred to you? Sketch a map of inhabitants for one of these. Who lives there? What interactions do you have with the inhabitants? Titles. Draw the lines of interaction between inhabitants of this place.

3. Following impulse and imagination, sketch or collage a garden that you inhabit with other creatures. Who lives there? What interactions do you have with them? Title the stories.

BECOMING INHABITANTS

How different it seems to "inhabit" a place than to "occupy" it. "Occupy" has echoes of taking over: occupying a country, occupying a room; even people are "occupied," inaccessible to others. Inhabit, on the other hand, is about being in a "habitat," and reminds me that I am connected to the place where I live. There is a familiarity, an at homeness, about habitat; it is, after all, related also to habit. Animals, birds, plants — all have "natural habitats" and, in these, they have their own "niche;" they are part of a natural balance.

In a very basic sense, power is about inhabiting space. For several millennia, however, power has been equated with dominance and control, with "occupying" rather that "inhabiting." To inhabit space is to become part of the habitat whether it is our body, our house, our country, or our universe. An inhabitant is in relationship with place.

I inhabit the west dormer of an attic in an eighty year old, Portland style, four-story frame house that faces a busy city street. There are four dormers, each toward one of the four directions, a perfect cross. The attic is under construction. That is a primary reality here. My clothes hang in the north dormer on an alder stick from the forest suspended between two step ladders because the walls are not yet finished, anywhere. Still, it is a luxury to be able to hang clothes. At first there was only floor in the center of the cross. In the bathroom, the south dormer, temporary boards rocked over the floor joists when you walked to the bathtub, or sat on the toilet. Now there is a shiny vinyl floor in that dormer and even sheet rocked walls. There are still areas, however, in the outer reaches under the ceiling slope, where there is no floor and sometimes no ceiling. And, although we are working toward a kitchen, the only source of water is still the bathtub.

The West dormer, where I am most at home, is about eight feet by eight feet; most of this area is filled with the futon where I sleep and read and dwell. Outside my dormer window are the tip most branches of an eighty year old cherry tree. This year the branch that almost touches my window burst into white blossoms a week before the rest of the tree. It is a wonderful tree with a large, gnarly trunk and a squirrel in residence. As I look out the window, I can look across the rooftops of the neighborhood, and in the morning, Portland's skyscrapers against the horizon, reflect back the light of the rising sun. In the evening, the sun disappears behind the city, and I am, in my imagination, at my other home — walking the beach at Hug Point or Manzanita, as the sun turns the ocean silver and gold, then disappears down under.

Around me in my dormer are images of some of those who are special to me. A butterfly, a lady bug, a mountain goat, an owl. From the center of the ceiling, which is the inner slope of the roof, hangs a mobile of iridescent stars. Often in her cycle across the night sky, the moon passes across my window. Last night was a half moon night; white light filled the dormer, and here, above the rooftops, I was bathed in moonlight. When the moon is full, I am awake with the light most of the night.

Along with my good friend Rhia, a blue-eyed husky-malamute lunatic named Luna, and a feisty calico cat named Aunt Ellen, I have lived in this attic for two years, since it was bare bones. There are many stories the four of us could tell about the experience of living in one space with no walls and doors, no kitchen or kitchen sink, and barely a floor. The attic, like just about everything else in my life right now, is in the process of creation. I was surprised, however, to notice as I write this, how much I have become an attic inhabitant.

 ## Inside/Out

Create an inner space for yourself. What outward form does it take?

 ## From the Inside

In your imagination, sense a space from the inside — the inside of your heart, the inside of a cloud, the hollow of the oak tee, the inside of your drum. Sketch with words or color and shape.

 ## Space Play

Space play for the child self: create a space around you — a bed house, a fern house, a blanket cocoon. Let your senses become aware of what it feels like to be inside of this space. Where are the edges of the space? Draw its outer shape.

The Temple of the Soul

A Journey of Imagination:

Be sure you are in a comfortable, safe space. Breathe, ground, release tension.

See yourself walking along a path through a beautiful forest. As you walk, you hear the birds singing, the song of waters, and the wind stirring the tree branches high above you. Continuing along the forest path, you become aware of the faint sound of music. You are drawn toward the music; it is the most beautiful music you have ever heard. You yearn toward the sound as it grows clearer and clearer until you are at the entrance of a temple. Doves flutter, softly circling in the trees of the garden. As you enter, the music is all around you, filling the temple with sound. Allow yourself to dwell here, slowly become aware of the inside of the temple and how it feels around you.

When you are ready, give thanks with your heart for the beauty of this place. When impulse guides you, leave the temple and continue your walk along the forest path, listening to the sounds, aware of what is around you. When you are ready, breathe yourself back to present space.

Journaling: Catch the essence of the temple you experienced with either words or sketching.

 ## SITTING IN YOUR POWER

Coyote, in Karok Indian story, is so overcome with laughter at Spider Woman spinning rope from her "butt" that time and again he cracks up laughing. Finally Spider Woman cuts the rope that could save him and lets him fall, flat, in the Nevada desert. As Susan Strauss says in retelling the story, it's a very hard place to fall. Spider, like woman, gives birth from her butt. It is really her belly, but it looks like her butt to coyote.[4]

When I first heard this story, I knew it mirrored something very personal for me. Very early the laughter cut me from my intuitive, butt knowing. As a child I didn't know that this dismissal of feminine knowing and creating had been going on for millennia. I simply forgot how to listen to the wells within me. I learned how to survive and succeed in school and in my profession. I learned analysis, logic, speed, organization. But never very well. I kept the secret feeling that I was "not very smart." I know now that I birth by listening to what is passing through me. I can feel the pulse of it stirring within me. Then the restlessness will take me to some still place where I can go down deeply to listen and open to the birth. Sometimes it is a long birthing. Sometimes it is short. But it does not happen from figuring it out.

Perhaps this is why I so love the goddesses of Paleolithic and Neolithic peoples. Pregnant, round, they sit upon the earth, or as an image from Catal Huyuk, on the birthing throne. In Neolithic times, people shaped thrones, on top of the sacred mountain, the mountain of Her full belly. Throne meant "the lap of the goddess" in Egypt, where images show the pharaoh, fully grown and crowned, held nursing as an infant on the lap of the goddess. She is the source of his power.

The imagery surrounding the king is first that of a "gardener;" he is responsible for nurturing vegetation by his union with the goddess. Later (with animal herding cultures) he is a shepherd of the people. If you follow the evolution of this meaning further, however, the power is no longer connection, but power *over*, as "Divine Right" to rule.

In a Sumerian image (2000 BCE) the king holds a measuring rod and line for the building of the moon god's shrine.[5] I like to think that this sacred work of the hands was the first meaning of "ruler." He also holds the ring of the goddess. Barbara Walker comments that "it is still customary for rulers to hold the 'phallic' scepter in the right hand, the 'yonic orb' in the left, symbolizing the king's marriage to the goddess" (heiros gamos).[6]

There is, then, both a right hand and left hand of power, symbolizing the marriage between masculine and feminine. In this particular image, however, the king holds what appears to be an axe in his left hand and *both* a yonic ring and a measuring rod and line in his right. The image reflects the masculine domination over feminine that occurs at about this time in Sumerian history and that is also recorded in the 4,000 year old myth, *Inanna,* and in *The Epic of Gilgamesh.*

This image, which appears in the Wolkstein and Kramer edition of
Inanna, shows the king and the goddess sitting on either side of the tree
of life. The king holds a measuring rod and line, emblems of rulership
and the ring of the goddess. He also holds an axe. (2,000 BCE)

The image is, however, a composite, created from the two pieces
in the photograph shown here. The originals do not show a friendly
exchange. They show the king replacing the goddess on the
throne of power, receiving the devotion of the people.

Artist Buffie Johnson describes a Minoan snake bird goddess who, she says, is
probably related to the Dactyls of Mt. Ida, a group of Shamanic women who personi-
fied the divine use of the hands. In this image of the goddess, She is holding up both
her right and left hand, which are very different in appearance. The long slender
left hand, says Johnson, belongs to the sorceress; the broad right hand is male. "This
is consistent with the tradition of the right hand as doer and the feminine left as the
hand of wisdom."[7]

In order to find balance, we must claim both hands of power. Since the words
"right" and "left" have so frequently been associated with positive versus negative
meanings (right as "correct"; left as sneaky or sinister) I suggest thinking of this
polarity as "doer" and "knower" or "sender" and "receiver."

The Two Hands of Power

1. Sitting in a comfortable and safe place, breathe and let go of tension. With eyes closed, hold up your hands in the Dactyl Goddess pose. What do your hands look like, feel like? Focus on each one separately, sensing its image and feeling what it likes to do.

2. Imagine that you are holding a yonic symbol (such as a ring) in the left hand and a phallic symbol (such as a rod or scepter) in the right. Notice how this feels and what the symbols look like.

3. When you are ready, sketch your left hand and your right hand. How would you describe the differences? Does one feel superior to the other? Sketch the symbols you held.

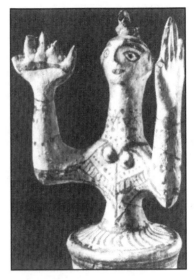

Dactyl goddess with right and left hands of power raised in blessing (Minoan, 1400 BCE)

Strengthening The Hands

Dwelling and Listening

Practice "dwelling." Choose, for instance, something to dwell with for a week or more — a symbol, or a stone, or a shell, or an image. Look at it, sense it, allow it into your consciousness. Practice posing questions about it and listening for the answers. Be willing to surrender expectation and listen. Giving significance to what you discover by writing or sketching, will strengthen this way of knowing.

Deciding and Doing

1. Make a list of the creative projects you have imagined "someday doing."

2. Choose the one you are most attracted to and work further with it: what do you need in order to begin? What is the first step?

3. What feelings come up when you think about doing the project? (doubts, fears, excitement, futility…)

4. Make a list of the strengths you have for accomplishing the project.

5. What do you need from the people around you? Who will support and encourage you in the project? Who will feel pleased with your accomplishment?

6. In your mind's eye, see the project as it grows to completion. What does it look like? Feel your satisfaction and pride.

7. Write a letter to a friend about the successful completion of the project or write a news bulletin using third person (your name, he/she). If the project will be marketed, present it in an advertisement.

〰〰〰〰〰〰〰〰〰〰〰〰〰〰〰

 ## GRANDMOTHER OAK

In my old neighborhood, among the contemporary homes and immaculate lawns, were a few old oak trees, survivors from the woods that had once grown there. One of these, a massive tree, took up the whole yard of a white colonial house. I loved looking into the expanse of branches and imagining their mirror image, its root system beneath the earth.

I worried that the man who owned the house would cut the tree down as people in the neighborhood often did to prevent leaves from falling on their lawns. Sometimes I counted twenty or thirty garbage bags of leaves in his yard. Once, I told him of my worry. He replied that he lived there *because* of the tree. After that, he always apologized to me when he had to prune its branches.

One night I paused in front of the tree and posed a question about my work. It was an important question for I was at a crossroads where a decision had to be made. As I stood, feeling her black oak shape against the sky, I heard the answer clearly: "Root deeply. Love the mother. And branch."

For a moment I felt the immensity of the oak within me, her depth, strength, height. Since that night, I have cherished the gift of this mantra. Again and again, it has taken me through confusion to the simplicity of center. I call it the Oak Mantra.

To "ground" is to open your "root" and feel your connection with earth. Grounding is only mysterious in that we have forgotten this connection. When we relax into and open our root, we allow the Kundalini "snake" of energy to flow down into earth. These living roots connect us to earth's nurturance. This snake of energy can also flow back up the roots, up the tree, and fly from the branches as bird (mind, spirit).

The awareness of this energy movement up and down the spinal tree has existed for a long time. This is apparent from the number of "snake-bird" goddesses in our mythic heritage, including Inanna, Isis, Athena, and Eurynome. The "tree of life," stylized into the caduceus, is still used as the AMA and Chiropractic logo, symbolizing balance and health. The god Hermes, millennia earlier, held the caduceus as his alchemical staff of life.

That the lower half of our bodies has been considered inferior to the upper and that the snake has been condemned as evil, simply show us how deeply we have been severed from our root source, the earth. The root center of the body, says Anodea Judith, has the same vibrational frequency as the earth.[8] When the energy is relaxed and flowing in this center, we feel "at home," connected to our power.

▼ *Grounding*

A Journey of Imagination

Find a comfortable, safe place to sit, where you will be uninterrupted. Your back should be straight, your legs uncrossed. You may wish the back support of a chair or wall; outside, a tree or a rock.

First, breathe in and out, simply to relax your body and release tension. Become aware of the weight of your body against the earth, or chair, or floor. To become more conscious of your root, try rocking back and forth or in a circle, feeling your bottom against the floor. As your body relaxes, feel the warmth growing at the base of your spine, a glowing egg of energy.

Now, on the exhale, visualize the breath flowing down your body and out in a root that pushes downward, feel the desire of your root to push deeply into the earth. Your roots may branch as you go more deeply still. Continue to breath deeply and exhale down through your roots into the earth.

When your roots break through into "the center of the earth," you will experience a flood of warm energy. Allow yourself to be effortlessly in this place. You are floating in a lake of milk at the heart of the Mother, being washed and filled, washed and filled. Stay in this place as long as you wish. When you are ready, use your in-breath to draw up vibrant energy. Feel the roots going down from your body; the warm earth energy flowing back up, filling your body and pushing out in branches from your crown.

When you are ready, slowly bring your self back to present by focusing on breath. After awhile, you will be able to ground most anywhere, on the bus, at a dinner party, during an interview. When you are grounded, you sit in the throne of your power.

MOVEMENT 4

Receiving The Gifts of Feminine Wisdom

For the cosmos, memory is the way the past works in the present.
BRIAN SWIMME,
The Universe is a Green Dragon

 ## THE EYE OF MEDUSA

I sat in a talking circle of about twenty men and women. We were asked to speak of what needed to happen to heal the wound between women and men, between masculine the feminine, between earth and people. "We must find the balance in ourselves," one woman said. "We must not blame," said another; "we must focus on our love, not our anger." "We must forget the past," spoke a young man, "and focus on the future." I felt the rage rising within me. I could not speak. I rose and walked outside.

I stood on the porch of the conference building, breathing the cool, spring air and remembering. I remembered the words of the young Indian woman who the night before had told personal stories of native people all over the earth, people who are saying "No." "No, you cannot take this land. I will not move my home so that you can clear-cut, strip mine, nuclear test..." She, herself, standing before the board of Exxon, saying No. I remembered how she spoke of the number, a six digit number, that identifies her as a government ward. I remembered the pain, the radiance of her face as she spoke of her love for her people and for this earth.

I remembered the astonishment and, sometimes, the disbelief of my mythology classes when they discover as Merlin Stone puts it that once "god was a woman." My students call me "feminist" for teaching of the 25,000 years of mythology before patriarchal domination. "Alright," I say to them, "that's fine. But what about those who remember only the last 5,000 years, claiming the rest of our story doesn't exist or is of no significance? Do you call them masculinists?"

Then there are others, the ones who, like me, can't believe they did not know, those that it changes forever. I remember my outrage in discovering I had not been taught what really happened to the Native cultures on this continent even though I had many years of education. I remember in the seventies being told by a professor with a Ph.D. that there was no evidence of matrifocal cultures. I had begun to suspect. I had begun to ask the question. I had begun to see the evidence in myths like *The Epic of Gilgamesh* which records the mythic moment when the hands of "man" turn against the earth and the goddess. In this myth you feel the blow that Gilgamesh strikes with his 600 pound ax, killing the guardian of the ancient cedar forest that once grew in the land now called Iraq. At this moment, we are told, the magic is scattered to the winds and chaos ensues. The goddess Ishtar rages at the violation — and is called a "bitch."

"This woman is angry," my students say of Barbara Walker when they read her *Woman's Encyclopedia of Myths and Secrets*. "Yes." "Now listen to what she says. Why is she angry?" I reply. I remember my own outrage when I discovered that I had not been told. I had not been told how much older my story is — not 5,000 years of culture but 30,000 years; not always a Father God but once a Great Mother, whose abundance and beauty encircled the people. There had not always been war; cultures had been at peace with each other and the earth — for thousands and thousands of years. I remember the outrage, the grief, I felt when I heard of the violence, the wars, the burning and raping of cultures — the obliterating of memory. In the stories of these people which are only now being remembered, I hear my own human story. I hear the pain. I feel the strength, rooted so deeply in the past, that now grows in me.

The face of Medusa rises before me, contorted in rage, fiery eyes defiant, piercing through the lies, hair writhing in snakes of passion. My own face merges with hers: she is my her-storical rage. She is my rage that this violation continues into the present. She is my face as my eyes freeze the eyes of my lover who has thrown me to the floor in his rage and holds me there, overpowering me with physical strength. "And is this who you are?" she asks him. Her eyes, her voice, fearsome to him. Her hair writhes from her head in angry snakes. Later, he tells her that in mythology Medusa is killed so Athena will never have such ugly energy again.

Still she rises. She must speak the truth or her passion consumes her. She is a face of power. She is "me" wisdom, wisdom born of experience. She is the passion that rises like flame from experience; she is the truth that experience teaches. Her name is also Medicine, for she is a healing fire. Me, the root of her name, is connected to mother and Maat and matter.

No. She will not forget. She is just remembering. Remembering her right to her rage. Remembering her right to her grief. Remembering, even, that she has the right to remember. The memories send her roots deep and strong. From them, she says "No" to present violation. It must stop. She will not forget to remember.

Remembering Not to Forget

1. What do you choose not to forget.

2. Which of these memories do you choose to pass on to the children? Create the way you will pass it on: if a story or a painting, what is its title; if a ritual, what is its name; if a song, what is its refrain?

EASTER IN THE MANZANITA LAUNDROMAT

Rattling the door to the Laundromat, I had the cold realization that my blankets, my only blankets, were locked inside. "How did the door get locked?" I puzzled. I had only been gone for a few minutes walk on the beach. Suddenly the door opened and Luna and I were inside a brightly lit Laundromat occupied by two sub-teenage boys. The boys were dressed "cool;" they talked about Elvis Presley songs and began entertaining themselves with Luna's reel leash — whipping it from one end of the Laundromat to the other. Luna looked me seriously in the eyes and began letting me know very loudly in Malamute howls that this was outrageous. Was I going to put up with it?

Just then, the conversation shifted. "Tomorrow is Easter," one said. "It is the day God died." "No," said the other, "It is when the rabbit lays eggs." A brief discussion followed and I realized that I was being asked the question: "Do rabbits really lay eggs?" "No, of course not," I said. It is one of the few times I have resisted a mythological discussion. There was less than a moment's pause before the boys loaded themselves into the dryers for a Saturday night spin.

Easter Day, the sun filtered through the mists of the forest. I had decided to celebrate Easter in a place I call "The Green Man Grotto." In this place, a small stream, born of a spring a few hundred feet up the mountain dwells for a moment in a forest pond, then pours into a clay cauldron and disappears into the earth. It flows underground, through the roots of two giant cedar, and emerges again fifty feet later. On a cedar tree hangs a mask from Bali. The Green Man I call him. He has geckos that look like the forest salamanders on his cheeks and he is very green.

Green Man Grotto,
Wanderland Rainforest

The Laundromat conversation had been floating in and out of my mind. "Perhaps it is not such bad mythology after all," I thought. For me, God did die. First the Father God died. Then, I was done with the patriarchal myth as well. And then, There was an even deeper death of god in me. It was long and painful and directly to the heart. My friends thought I would never stop grieving a relationship I, myself, chose to end. God died then, too, went back to ashes. I could no longer see him in the faces of men.

All over Manzanita that Easter morning, families were collecting the many colored eggs of spring born from the winter's death. Standing in the Green Man Grotto washed by the sunlight and the sound of waters, I, too, was collecting the gifts of spring. I sang to the green, the new green leaves, dancing in the forest light. I sang to the beauty of the green man dancing.

Green light moved between the leaves. In front of the great cedar, the light shifted and glowed. I looked, afraid to move or breathe, at a face, as real as the tree behind it, that looked back at me. It was, at first, gnarly and primal — a root god, an earth god, the face of Humbaba. Shifting and changing, the face became the radiantly beautiful face of god as man. Through the rainbow mists, spirit light glowed. It was a light I had seen in the face of my lover. For a moment the face became the face of my lover in his greatest beauty and the familiar grief began to break through me.

But then it was not my lover's face, but coyote's that laughed out at me as if to say "just thought I'd try that old trick on you one more time! Almost got you, too!"

"No," I said, as the illusion melted away in the still shifting light. "Your beauty is great, but god did not die when you died in me." I stood in the green gold light, the presence of the god radiant around me. I stood there for a long time, until I could sustain it no longer. Then, I turned to go.

"God, too, can be recreated." The words floated through me. This was my gift from the Green Man on Easter Day. I left a white onyx egg in the moss under the gaze of the Green Man mask: "To the Great Hare who lays the eggs of creation; may we collect and re-collect."

 ## Fertile Soil

The goddess Rhea, the story goes, placed her hands on the fertile earth. From the fingers of her right hand sprouted the gods, and from the fingers of her left hand sprouted the goddesses.

Sit quietly for a few moments, breathing and grounding. Place your hands on a large sheet of paper (black roofing paper works well). See your highest aspirations of the feminine flowing from the fingers of your left hand, see flowing from the fingers of the right hand, your highest aspirations of the masculine.

Using finger-paints, colored chalk, or crayons, sketch what you saw. Name the gods and goddesses.

 ## Re-Creating

1. How did you see your body when you were ten years old? 15? 21? now? Re-create your image to please you.

2. What image do you have of yourself at age 85? Freewrite whatever comes. Then choose how you wish to re-create the image.

3. Free associate with the headings "men," "women." Then choose how you wish to re-create the image.

4. What image of masculine and feminine would you choose to pass on to others, especially to children?

 ## DRINKING FROM THE STREAM OF TIME

> *I know I hung on that windy tree,*
> *Swung there for nine long nights,*
> *Wounded by my own blade,*
> *Bloodied for Odin,*
> *Myself an offering to myself:*
> *Bound to the tree*
> *That no man knows*
> *Whither the roots of it run.*[1]

Odin, from Norse Mythology, is a sky god who inhabits the top most branches of the World Tree. Many sky gods feel superior to earth, much like mind tends to feel superior to body. But Odin is drawn to storm, to clouds racing across the night sky split by lightning. Perhaps this passion stirred in him desire, for Odin desired beyond the realm of most sky gods.

Odin wanted to drink from the stream of Time. He wanted memory. He knew it would be painful; he knew he wouldn't always be in control of memory. Still, he desired its gifts so much that he was willing to give one of his eyes so he could look inward.

Some fear the pain of memory and choose not to recollect. They become, as Joanna Macy puts it, "psychically numb." Others crucify themselves with the pain of the past; they cannot see beyond it. They tell it over and over; they suffer over their suffering. It is a powerful drink, this gift of memory.

When Odin drinks of time, he becomes human: he experiences change and death. The tree of life is continually growing and changing and dying and seeding again. This is the cyclic continuity of life. Women experience growing and dying as a cycle natural to their bodies and connected to the larger rhythms created by earth and moon. Not only does their menstrual cycle follow a process similar to the moon's waxing and waning, it is pulled by "moon time" through a monthly cycle.

This in-body knowing of the life cycle is a *feminine* mystery. The lineage of the word "menstruation" from *men*, month and moon, tells us how deeply this is a feminine experience. Odin's story, however, is a male initiation story. In this story, "sacrifice" means to be wounded, to suffer, to bleed on the "cross of life."

Odin is hung on the tree for nine nights. The birthing time was spoken of as "nine-night" in folk language."[2] It was a sacred time. From the birthing blood and waters, from the pain and letting go, new life was born. It was a time "to make sacred." This is the core meaning of the word "sacrifice" (sacre/sacred; fice/make). Odin experiences "dying to himself." Like the moon (or the snake, or the woman) he "sheds his skin."

In patriarchal language, "a spear in the side" becomes an important symbol of sacrifice. In meaning and practice "sacrifice" then shifts from "making sacred" the cycle of birthing and dying to the experience of pain and suffering. In the image of Odin "hung" on the cross of life, we receive two important mythic imprints simultaneously: first, that he *is* initiated — as he dies to himself, he "sees" the runes, the words of wisdom rising from the depths of his consciousness — and, that wounding and suffering are necessary. In the feminine cycle, bleeding is the experience of shedding or letting go. The archetype of the Odin story — that wounding and bleeding are necessary for sacrifice — easily moves into a warrior/war mythology. It is hard to understand why one would choose to pass on a mythology that focuses on wounds and wounding and that creates suffering.

Still, Odin is initiated into feminine mystery; he becomes part of a larger cycle of dying/birthing. This is evident in another detail of his mythology: the horse he rides across the stormy sky is named after Spider and is associated with the spinning of fate. There is a place where we must surrender, the myth tells us. There is a place where we are "the woven ones." And this can be painful, can be filled with passion, like an Odin thunderstorm.

This gift of memory that Odin receives is, then, most definitely a mixed blessing, and one of my favorite things about Odin is how much he cherishes it. One story about him shows how this mixture works. After drinking from time, Odin has a worry problem. He now knows that things get lost, and end, and die and that sometimes it hurts a lot. He can't forget this. And he also knows he can't stop it from happening.

One morning Odin sat in the top branches of The World Tree, thinking and worrying. The World Tree was huge. Its roots went deeply back into time, through generations of peoples, and cultures, through the changing millennia of earth itself to the very belly of beginnings. The branches of the World Tree grew far into the heavens and vanished from human sight. Every morning, it was Odin's custom to send out his two ravens, Thought and Memory. "Fly to the earth," he would tell them; "bring me back the news, bring me back the stories." Each evening the ravens would return, and far into the night they would tell the stories of earth — stories about birthing, about loving, about dying. Stories about suffering and about courage. Stories of desire and of beauty.

Then one day, a worry filled Odin's mind, "What if..." "What if some day one of my ravens does not return? If one of the ravens should perish," he thought," which one could I live without?" For a long time, he sat brooding. When he spoke, the leaves trembled in the winds. "I fear for my thought, lest he not return; but even more I fear for my memory."[3]

Odin's story set me pondering: what would be lost with Memory? The wisdom that comes by learning from experience. The memory of people who have died before me: my uncles and aunts, and grandparents. My mother. The smell of my grandfather's peach orchard. The memory of my grandfather's love. The pain of parting from a lover. The memory of the lover. The memory of his touch. The memory of cultures and peoples before me. The memory of their pain. The memory of their gifts to me. The memory of my own changing and growing. The memory of my daughter in the moment of her marriage, as the time-wheel in my mind spun backwards and I held her, a baby in my arms. My mind floods with memory.

 ## Sensory Rivers

Taking one at a time, allow each of your senses to become a river of memory:
The sound of...
The smell of...
The touch of...
The taste of...
The movement of...
The sight of...

 ## Elemental Memories

Select one memory to cherish
from what you have known of water
from what you have known of earth
from your experience of sky
from your knowing of fire

 ## Whacks of Fate

1. When were the times when something happened "to you" that changed your life? (Don't puzzle about this. Jot down whatever comes to mind.)
2. To find the "gifts" of fate, write the event in the center of a page and collage around it with words or images — what has grown from this happening?
3. Make a list of the titles of teachings or lessons you have received from fate.

 ## The Spinning of Fate

Each of us is born upon a time. Spinning out from the belly of Grandmother Spider, we ride the filaments, in that moment born — of the universe, of the planet, of our culture, of our parents — into a particular place. These imprints are our birthing "garment," the cloak we are given. Then our own weaving and reweaving begins.

Universal Cloak: First do some sketching. What season were you born into? What weather? Was it day or night? Dusk or dawn? What stars and moon? What place on the earth — mountains, forest, plains, rivers, desert...

From your sketching, create the cloak you wore when the universe birthed you into time and place. Use color, yarn, fabric, feathers, images, pictures (drawn or clipped) to create the patterning. Let this take whatever form that seems natural. Or tell it with words.

Cultural and Familial Cloak: Write down the date and place of your birth at the top of a page. List the major forces or imprints of this time and place. For instance, some of the major imprinting forces of my birth time and place were economic depression, war, patriotism, moral ethic, work ethic, male dominance, importance of marriage and nuclear family—and Oregon country—farms, small town, and wilderness. (This may be more an exercise of what you know than what you remember.)

One way to see your cultural cloak from a distance is to sketch it like a circular web: The center is your self and the first circle the time place of your birth. The concentric circles moving out from center are the rings of your aging and place (five years, ten years, fifteen years...). The spokes radiating out from the center are the major imprinting forces. Put in the "Whacks of Fate" by giving each a symbol.

Use color and texture to indicate where the imprints were deepest, and how they felt. If you like, add images by sketching or collaging.

 ## *Reweaving Your Cloak*

1. Start a list of attitudes and values that you were given in your cultural and familial cloaks. (For example, I was given the imprint that physical beauty was of great importance for a woman, and that if she was not in relationship with a man, she was not whole.)

2. From your list, choose one thought that still affects you. Put it in the center of the page and free associate around it, letting images, emotions, memories flow onto the page. Don't censor. Notice what this thought has magnetized to it: what kinds of emotions? What kinds of images? What you see around it is the power, the effect, the thought has on you. Deeply imprinted thoughts are sometimes called "thought-forms" because they shape, or form, reality.

3. If you choose not to keep this thought about reality, "trade it in" for one that you do wish to cultivate. (For instance, I appreciated the reversal this thought gave to a thought-form I have about personal clumsiness: "Anything worth doing is worth doing clumsily at first.")

4. Write out the new thought and again free-associate around it to see what kind of cloak you are weaving. To deepen the new imprint, use images (collaged or sketched) to remind you of this new way of seeing.

 ## WEAVING THE PATTERN OF REALITY

A poetry text I was using for a class defined ballads as songs or poems that pass on stories of courage, romance, and action. Yet, every story had themes of violence, murder, robbery, fear, and war. A woman poisoned her lover with eel stew; a jealous lover shot a rival; a woman betrayed her lover to the army; a great train robber was betrayed and murdered by a friend. Is this, then, what "action, romance, and courage" have come to mean? We pondered this question in class.

"It seems that way in the movies, too," the class pointed out.

"Is this what you want to pass on to your children?" I asked them. I mentioned recently seeing Lou Gold's passionate slide show, "Lessons from the Ancient Forest." In it, he reminds us of a Native American teaching: make your decisions for seven generations of children who follow you.

Granny, in Anne Cameron's *Daughters of Copperwoman,* says it takes four generations "to get people's heads fixed" after killing their own kind — and we haven't even had one generation. (People) get jerked around inside somehow, and it takes a long time to get right again."[4] How many generations does it take before violence is imprinted in genetic memory, before "the nature of man is violent"? Some say that this is so already. "There have always been wars," they say. One of my students tells me after our class discussion, "Come back to reality!"

"It is not a reality that I choose," I answer. "Why should I? Who would want to live in fear and violence and war?"

There is a difference between remembering our story and glamorizing a story of fear and violence. There is a difference between learning the lessons of experience and passing on what is destroying us.

What are the yarns we choose to spin? What are the patterns we choose to weave for our children? Through the violence and the pain, the wisdom stories are passed on by generations of women in *Daughters of Copperwoman.*

> *With her loom and with her broom*
> *with her love and with her patience*
> *she weaves the pattern of destiny*
> *and sweeps beaches and minds,*
> *She weaves the pattern of reality*
> *and tidies shorelines and souls.*[5]

 Keeper of the Family Stories

1. What personal and family stories of courage, love, and action would you choose to pass on to your children?

2. Give them titles to keep their memory and arrange them in a Table of Contents for your Family Story Book. Have family story telling sessions, letting the children choose the story to be told from the Table of Contents.

3. Encourage the children to add their own story titles and become story tellers. Arrange them in a Table of Contents for your *Family Story.* They might be called *Stories of The Youngers.*

ANIMAL RELATIVES

These are my animal relatives, my clan:
Bear, who teaches me the Mother Cycle
Honey Bee, who flew into me with vibration and sings a golden song
Humming Bird, whose quick sharp beak helps me make the mending stitches
Eagle, who first flew me to Her
Dove, who circles in flocks and drops her downy feathers in my home
Coyote, whose laughter echoes along my path
Owl, whose ears open me in the dark
Spider, who teaches me to weave
Snake, who swims the river of my body
And Wolf, who watches me through
    Luna's wild blue eyes...

 ## *Totem Tree*

Who are your animal relatives? Sketch them in words. Then create a Totem Tree by first sketching your tree of life and then letting your animals inhabit the tree. Follow impulse on where they would be and how to represent them.

 ## VIOLIN MAKER

It was a warm June afternoon in the forest. I had been working steadily most of the day — lifting logs, stacking, cutting brush — when my body suddenly registered zero energy.

I walked slowly down the hill to the creek and lay down in the sun, my body melting exhaustion into the earth beneath me, my mind drifting into the sound of water. The music brought me back to the surface of consciousness. It was the sweetest music I had ever heard — violin music. Violin music so beautiful my whole body filled with bliss as I lay motionless — listening, just listening, there on the earth by the creek at Wanderland. Even when I could hear the music no longer, I lay motionless for a long time. Then filled with an inexplicable joy, I walked back up the hill.

I had no idea how to explain what I had experienced. There are no neighbors nearby nor was this music like any I had heard before. Some time later, I received a letter from the former owners of this place, telling of its earliest settlers: "There used to be an old house (but not in our time) below the bridge. It was owned by a man named Handy. Mason said he made and played violins and you could hear him playing all through the valley in the evening..."

I like to think of this violin maker each evening playing to the valley, playing to the waters, playing to the winds. How he must have known this place: the rushing of water in the winter, the waves of wildflowers in the spring and early summer, the elk and deer shyly listening in the evening light. How he must have loved the music he played to the waters, violin music blending with the evening bird songs.

I like to think how deeply earth remembers and sings back our songs. I like to think that more and more people are hearing the voice of earth's memory. Not long ago, I sat in the middle of a crowded room listening to the voices all around me. The room was filled with women sharing good food and stories about their lives here on the Oregon coast. I was hearing snatches of a conversation near me: "One place in the forest I heard the sound of drumming..." "I can feel, on my land, what happened there before me..." For a moment, I wasn't sure I had understood correctly: "You are talking about hearing the earth?" I asked. Then we were all sharing our stories.

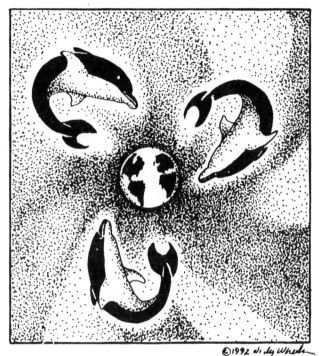

Earth Song
Winky Wheeler

 Keeper of Earth Story

1. Collect the stories of a place that is special to you. Start with the stories you already know. Talk to people who have lived there a long time about what they remember. Titles may be all you need especially if you pass the stories on by story telling. Arrange the titles in a Table of Contents for *The Story of This Place* book.

2. Spend time with this place; dwell there. Be in an attitude of listening. Surrender expectation. Hearing may come as impressions, feelings, thoughts, vision, sounds... Write, sketch, draw these stories and include them in *The Story of This Place* book.

ANCESTOR

Yesterday I walked across the stones of Wander Creek, Listening to the rapids under the overhanging cedar bows. This is a place I love, a place I have walked many times.

I stopped in front of an old cedar stump, logged one hundred years ago from the banks of this creek. Now she is a giant, red, decaying mother 12 feet across. New trees send their roots like snakes pushing down through her stump body into earth. For a moment I felt her full height still, saw her towering in the sky in front of me, felt her roots in my legs, deep and strong. She was so beautiful.

Then an impulse ran through me as if she said — "you think I am old..." With it, I turned and saw in the creek bed, veiled by cedar boughs, a rock that was different from the others. I parted the boughs of cedar and entered a place the earth, the cedar and the waters had shaped as special. Running under the bank and out again into a sheltered rapid pool, the waters sang.

In front of the rock, pure sand formed an island, a beach untouched. But the rock — the rock was a log, an ancient tree mother turned to stone. How old was she? From what ancient tropical forest? A tree I cannot name that grew once, here, before even the mountain was born.

I felt with my hands the cold rock grain, the weight too heavy to move, and I sat there with this ancient ancestor, afraid to even imagine how deeply *her* roots go.

 ## *Remembering the Elders*

1. Sketch a tree that represents your life tree. In the roots put the names of the elders who have supported and given strength to your life. Try two drawings, one to see "foremothers;" the other "forefathers" (remember that these are not necessarily "blood relatives"). Consider the possibility of a photo collage.

2. Under the branches place the names of those whom your tree of life shelters and nourishes.

FOR THOSE YET UNBORN...

I am Dekanawideh and with the chiefs of the Five Nations
I plant the Tree of the Great Peace...

Roots have spread out from the Tree of the Great Peace...
The Great White Roots of Peace...

Any person of any nation
may trace the roots to their source and be welcome
beneath the Great Peace...

We bind ourselves together
by taking hold of each other's hands...

Our strength shall be in union
our way the way of reason
righteousness and peace...

Think not so much of present advantage
as the future welfare of the people...

Think not forever of yourselves nor of your own generation

Think of those yet unborn whose faces are coming from beneath the ground...[6]
from *The Tree of The Great Peace* (c. Iroquois 1450)

Memory

Using images (draw, collage, write, sculpt) create a "memory" to pass on to those "whose faces are coming from beneath the ground."

Time Capsule

Create a "capsule" of artifacts that might be found millennia from now. What would you pass on as a memory of your life, your time and place?

Attracting Possibilities

Formerly the future was simply given to us; now it must be achieved. We must become the agriculturists of time. If we do not plant and cultivate the future years of human life, we will never reap them....

JONATHAN SCHELL, *The Fate of the Earth*

 ## A WOMAN SAW

A few years ago (I guess you could say "Once upon a time...) a woman saw — and what she saw was painful. She saw a planet dying: the people dying, the animals dying, the forests and the waters and the atmosphere dying. Perhaps she was watching TV when she saw; perhaps she was driving down the freeway, or perhaps she was deep in meditation — but she saw. She asked in prayer; she asked in ritual; she asked in thought: how can these hands help?

Twice she dreamt. She was speeding down the freeway when she suddenly turned to the left and down a gravel road as far as she could drive. She was in a forest by a rushing stream. The water was so high she could go no farther. She parked the car and began walking along a path. She walked past a beautiful home, lit with soft lights, with warmth and magic. As an outsider, she walked by her own home.

She walked on. Then she saw the shed. It was primitive, straw on the floor. She thought animals must live there. She walked further, down into a chamber where a woman was teaching of "squaring the circle." She didn't know what this meant (nor did she know when she woke up). But she stayed to listen. In the dream she didn't know why it was important to listen. She only knew it was important to listen.

Twice she dreamt. She was speeding down the freeway when she suddenly turned to the left and....

Time spun by, days and nights, weeks, and months. It was an early spring day — rainy and cold along the ocean. Her room at the motel was not ready, so she decided to just drive around awhile. Someday, she fantasized, she'd like to live out here, after she retired, and.... She turned left down a county road — hills and streams. Then the road ended and became a gravel country lane disappearing into a dense rainforest.

A "for sale" sign stood amidst the bushes. She parked the car and opened the door. The sound of rushing stream waters, the smell of damp earth — green.

It was on this day that the woman fell in love with a rainforest. It was on this day that her dream began to come into form. It was on this day that Wanderland was born.

She did not know, however, just how much work of the hands it would be to love a rainforest. Nor did she know how this love would change her, would change her life.

Dream Re-Runs

Dreams that "re-run" are insisting on being heard. What are your recurring dreams? View them as movies. Give them titles. Try writing thirty second reviews of them: this movie shows you…; this movie takes you….

THE POWER OF ASKING

Creation stories are about the *process* of creation. They tell in images and imagination what physicists tell in abstract equations. Both speak of primary laws and of energy movement. Both speak of interactions between polarities that generate energy and give birth to form.

Because mythology is a holographic language, however, creation stories not only describe the laws of universal birthing at the beginning of time but also the laws of creative birthing within you now. Sometimes these stories also show you primary "abilities," ways to participate in creativity.

This is a very personal and direct relevance that many prefer not to see in mythology. "But it is not *real*!" my students sometimes object, like the boy in the film, "Never Ending Story," who suddenly discovers that he is experiencing the myth he is reading about. To see for a moment, how strange this reaction is, try imagining a Paiute or a Hopi stopping in the middle of a sacred dance and saying "Wait a minute, this isn't real. What I am dancing, what I am singing, what I am feeling, has no relevance to my personal life, has no relevance to me."

The primary "laws" of creativity described in creation stories are very similar to what David Spangler calls the "laws of manifestation." They form an active process that follow this essential pattern: 1) feeling the stirring of desire, 2) allowing possibility, 3) focusing intent, 4) surrendering individual will to overall balance and healing, 5) giving thanks, and 6) doing the work. What is described is an active relationship between individual and cosmos. It is a relationship balanced, however, by polarities of questing and receiving, asking and listening, willing and letting go. This balance is found most frequently in the mythologies of Native Peoples because they live in relationship with the creative cycles of earth — of generation, death, and regeneration.

One of the most haunting legends of old European mythologies, on the other hand, shows the dis/ease that results when the balance is lost and only quest and question remain. In the myth of the Fisher King, a wounded king sits in his boat, fishing a silent sea for an answer: how can the sterile lands be healed? how can the sterile king be healed? T.S. Eliot made this image a central metaphor of his surreal portrait of twentieth century society, *The Waste Land*. The people of his poem live withered lives of desperation and boredom; their quests and questions have become more and more trivial. They avoid the regenerating rains, the waters that run deep; they no longer feel the stirring of their own desire. To lose touch with this vital center is to lose authenticity.

As the Fisher King motif evolves into the "grail legends," the sea, the regenerative center, is visualized as a sacred vessel that has been lost. But by this time, the king (severed from the earth and the feminine in himself) lies ill inside the castle as the knights pursue an answer that has been deeply forgotten. It is only through the younger self (the "fool") Perceval, who, as Campbell points out, lives close to his own "impulse system," that the answer can be remembered.[1] For the king to be healed, for the lands to be healed — the separation between the two must end.

Question and answer are magnetic polarities in a Zuni creation story. Twins of light are created, as to right and left; as to "question and answer in deciding and doing."[2] The myth gives the people a gift of clarity, an ability that can guide their actions: to ask and to listen.

To ask a question propels the arrow of intent. The more deeply desire moves in the question, the more strongly the answer is magnetized. It may rise, breaking through the surface of our knowing. It may come in a flash of inspiration or the comment of a friend. We cannot know how an answer might come, or even, what it might be. Often it is quite different from any of our preconceptions. We do know that there is a magnetism in the power of desiring and that we have the abilities to ask and to listen.

 ## Questing

Sending Out The Question:

Make a list of the questions you are currently asking most deeply in your life. Take the strongest one to focus on. Write it out or create it symbolically in a special way. There are many ways to do this: creating a symbolic collage; placing the question in symbolic form (stone, shell, feather...) on your altar or in a special place; tossing the question as a stone into a river or pool. Let your imagination lead you: send out the question, propelled by your intent.

Surrendering Expectation:

Let the question go. Perhaps imagine it as a vibration in the cosmic web, or as a current in the inner seas. Let go of your expectations about when the answer will come and about what the answer will look like. Be in an attitude of receptivity, of listening.

DANCERS

From the Mediterranean long ago comes this story of Eurynome who danced on the oceans of birth at the beginning of time. She was born out of the chaos, out of the womb of the primal seas. She was born on the heaves of the Great Mother whose belly moved with the tides of all possibility.

Egyptian Snake-Bird Goddess
(about 4000 BCE)

In the foam of the cresting waves, Eurynome danced. She danced and she danced, in the south wind she danced. She danced until she felt the winds moving, moving the waves of her body. Like a great snake, the winds moved through her body, until she crested like the waves and flew in the white rainbow light. She flew as a dove. She flew in the mists above the moving ocean. She flew in the currents, circling, until from her an egg was born.

The winds rose and like a serpent wrapped around the egg, seven times coiling and moving around the egg of life. In the rocking of the eternal seas, cradled by the winds of desire, the egg hatched and all creation was born — the stars and moon and sun and sky; the mountains and rivers and earth; the animals and birds and fishes and the people.

• • •

This goddess myth describes a different place of beginning than the later myths that start "In the beginning was the word..." In Eurynome are the moving waters, the stirring of desire that precedes naming. She is a "Snake Bird Goddess." As snake she goes deep. She moves through the waters, and through the earth, and through our bodies. As snake she moves in the winds of passion. And then she flies, moving now through states of being, of freedom, of bliss, of ecstasy, of peace.

Snake Bird Goddesses such as Eurynome remind us that at one time in our mythic heritage, sexual desire and spiritual bliss were not severed but "married." This was the essence of ancient Tantric goddess religions and is the root of Tantric yoga today.

From this heritage we also receive the image of The Tree of Life. For it is in the root of the tree, and in the root center of our spines that the Kundalini snake dwells. This snake of energy can uncoil and climb our spines, rising and cresting in our crowns, and fly as spirit ecstasy. This imagery is shown in portraits of gods and goddesses, especially in Mesopotamia, India, and Egypt. As a stylized image it is still used by the medical professions as a symbol of balance (the healing of dis/ease). The continued use of this image is particularly ironic, of course, in a culture that has tended to despise snakes, to cut down the trees, and to make sexuality profane.

The myth of Eurynome is about the stirring of desire. Desire is the source of creativity. The desire that moves through Eurynome, however, does not consume her, nor does it consume what is around her; it grows larger and larger until it flies and something new is born.

The Egg Is Hatching

My grandson, Jeremy, was two when he invented a game he called "The Egg is Hatching!" It was a time when he loved to play with the many different stones in and around my house. His favorite was a polished jasper egg as big as a hen's egg. It looked very much like a yin/yang egg with white swirling in one half and red in the other. It filled both his hands when he cupped them together.

Holding the egg in his hands, he would look at it with expectation, then excitement, and then in total glee he would scream "the egg is hatching!" Whatever we "saw," we would name: a yellow tailed purple butterfly! a giant frog with buck teeth! a beautiful rainbow! a box full of new toys! Jeremy never tired of the game.

Jeremy's game is an exercise in allowing possibilities. The most difficult part about it is suspending your self-conscious adult self to participate with the innocence of a child. It can be played with a friend or by yourself.

Choose a stone that feels good in your hand. Focus on one area of your life: for example, relationship or work. Breathe and ground. Hold the stone in your hands, feeling it grow full of potential and then fuller still. Then name what you see hatching. Sketch or write the Egg of Potential that you see.

If you are working with a friend take turns with the process. Speaking what you see as you see it brings it closer to manifestation.

DREAMERS

An Australian creation story tells of two primal dreamers who inhabit the sky and the earth. In the beginning, Wallanganda, the Milky Way, threw water on the earth, home of the great serpent, Ungud. Ungud swam with the waters, moving them deep.

And in the night, as Ungud and Wallanganda dreamt together, life arose from the watered earth in the form of their dreams. From the sky, from Wallanganda's dreaming with Ungud, images were projected onto rocks and cave walls, where they can still be seen. The images are painted without eyes or mouths. They are ancestral forms.

When their imprint had been made, Wallanganda multiplied their forms in the shape of living beings, which populated the earth. The earth serpent, Ungud, unfolding from within, gave each their rainbow body. From Ungud, they received eyes and mouths. From Ungud, they received their name and their individual story.

The serpent, Ungud, still dwells and dreams and awakes in the earth, dreaming with Wallanganda, dreaming with the spiraling stars of the Milky Way. From their dreaming comes creation.[3]

• • •

In Aboriginal imagination, this vortex of dreaming is imaged as concentric circles spiraling out from a continuously renewing center. Painted in the earth, this is the "soak," the place of emergence. From this place the ancestors came, leaving their footprints on the soft ground. This is the birthing place, the intersection between dreamtime and waking time. From the ancestral imprints grow the living beings.

Aboriginal languages have no word similar to the word "time;" instead, they describe the experience of consciousness.[4] The two primary realms of consciousness, dreaming and waking, are not separate from each other. They exist simultaneously, even though we may experience them separately. When the two are not separate, there is no way to view waking as superior to dreaming. From dreaming everything is born; to dreaming everything returns.

In Aboriginal ritual, when youth are initiated as keepers of the story, they are given a Tjuringa stone bearing the imprinted memory of the way back to center, back to source. This has the title: "Map of the Journeying of the Ancestors Back to the Dream-Time." The story teller holds the stone, and traces the spiral out from center back to center, playing the stone like a phonograph record — and so the story is spoken, spinning out from the Dreaming center.

Images, feelings, fantasies, thoughts are the seeds of creation. They are, in a sense, "the ancestors." From the spiral of our dreaming come the imprints of what we will bring into creation.

 ## Footprints

Create a "dream spiral." Using words or images make "imprints" of what you are dreaming into form.

 ## AT WANDERLAND

We have worked now for ten days clearing a strip of forest 100 x 30 feet for a septic drain field. We work tree by tree, log by log, using a chain saw, clippers, and hand saws. We saw and trim, carry and stack. Rotting wood from forests past also must be moved; sometimes it is many feet deep. We are thankful that there are few large trees. The oldest, a moss covered alder, fell with a deep thud, heavy against the earth. Our hearts hurt. We cut it into shorter lengths so we can plug it with Shitake spore and carry it into the forest to become alder mother.

"This is definitely Crone work," Rhia commented a few days into the project. Neither of us likes the cutting. We had hoped to avoid making this drain field by installing a composting toilet in this heavily rooted, water-shed area. The Department of Environmental Quality, however, said "No. Too experimental. Why would you want one of those when you can just flush it away?" It was an environmental attitude we ranked along with the state's forest management policy for clear-cutting the surrounding forests, leaving "two trees and two logs per acre for the wildlife."

I sometimes hear myself in frustration speaking over and over, like a bad-movie re-run, about the stupidity and unconsciousness of governmental bureaucracies. When this happens, my energy drains away in powerlessness. "What is the vision?" "What do I choose to work for," I remind myself.

Dirty and sweaty, and surrounded by stumps, we try not to feel discouraged, not to feel that we are participating in the destruction that now covers thousands of acres of the Oregon Coast Range. We work toward making Wanderland a forest farm, where gourmet mushrooms, blueberries, and lilies are grown using the methods of permaculture. We work to show the state that a forest can be profitable as a forest instead of a clear-cut and to keep the small portion of remaining rainforest directly behind Wanderland, here on Neahkanie Mountain, from becoming barren clear-cut.

Clearing even a small strip of rainforest by hand is hard and slow. I haul truck loads of rotting wood from the forest floor to become ground cover for the blueberry gardens. There, it will be spored with Stropharia to become a mushroom garden. We have a totemic relationship with beavers here at Wanderland. "Gnaw by gnaw. Don't get discouraged by looking at how big the job is," they remind us.

About mid-way in the clearing of the drain field, my way of seeing the process began to shift. "This will be the Wanderland garden," I thought for the first time. A front yard of lilies and blueberries. Flowering bushes. Butterflies, hummingbirds, and bees in the sunlight. My Crone hands, still in the process of cutting, began to create in my mind's eye — a forest garden.

I sat for a moment amidst the stumps to let the tiredness leave my body. Breathing and humming, I relaxed into the sunlight. A louder hum whirred by my head, and I saw a small bird perched on a hemlock twig barely a foot away. "Can't be a hummingbird," I thought, looking at it looking at me. Then she came, hovering just inches in front of my eyes, standing still in vibration. "Just breathe," I thought. My prayer rose with the breath, and for a moment, filled the current between us:

"Grandmother, sew up this wound. Stitch this overcoat with your quick beak. Grandmother, let my heart fly free. Grandmother, be with me." Then she was gone in a whir, into the clearing that was becoming the front yard garden at Wanderland.

"Prayers on the breath of the moment" I call these songs of response to earth or sky or bird or tree. I imagine that Native Americans would simply call them songs. In those moments it feels to me as if some part of creation comes forward to communicate with me. I think, however, that we open in response to each other. "Messengers" Evelyn Eaton says the Paiutes call them. In that moment of openness, they both bring the message and carry the message from us.

 ## Bad Movie Re-Runs

What are the "bad movies" that you re-run over and over? Give them titles. Review them. What are the people like? What are the situations like? How do they end? What part do you play in them?

Prayers on The Breath of The Moment

When were the moments today your song rose within you?

Make something to remind you of your song — and the "messenger" it connected you with.

THE ATTITUDE OF PRAYER

For years I have been in love with a prayer from the Navajo "Beauty Way" called "House Make of Dawn." It begins like this:

> *In Tsegihi (oh you who dwell!)*
> *In the house made of the dawn,*
> *In the house made of the evening twilight,*
> *In the house made of the dark cloud,*
> *In the house made of the he-rain,*
> *In the house made of the dark mist,*
> *In the house made of the she-rain,*
> *In the house made of pollen,*
> *In the house made of grasshoppers,*
> *Where the dark mist curtains the doorway,*
> *The path to which is on the rainbow,*
> *Where the zigzag lightning stands high on top,*
> *Where the he-rain stands high on top,*
> *Oh, Divinity!*
> *With your moccasins of dark cloud, come to us,*
> *With your leggings of dark cloud, come to us,*
> *With your shirt of dark cloud, come to us.*
> *With the dark thunder above you, come to us soaring.*
> *With the shapen cloud at your feet, come to us soaring.*
> *With the far darkness made of the dark cloud over your head;*
> *come to us soaring*

To know that we live within a house exquisitely woven in beauty is the "ground" of any prayer. To know that this house is alive — alive with Divinity — has been deeply forgotten. Out of the dis-ease created by our forgetting, our separation, has arisen a "new" science: ecology. The root of the word ecology, "ec," is house, as in "home economics." Ecology describes family relations within the household with the solidity of science. It allows us to understand how we are a household and why we are out of balance — in dis-ease.

At the same time, we are only remembering — for our ancestors knew by feeling the pulse of life in Earth: seeing the trees breathe mists, breathing the air fresh off the mountain stream; feeling the breath of earth in weather and seasons and cycles;

feeling the power of earth in floods and volcanoes and storms. In some places they called her Gaia. Now many speak her name again as an hypothesis newly discovered. Is the Earth alive? they ask, as if just waking from a long sleep of forgetting.

To live in a "house made of dawn" is to be alive in a living world. It is also to be at home in our household. When we remember ourselves in this household, we become aware that "it" is alive, and as Joseph Campbell says, we stop referring to "Nature" with the pronoun "it" (which denotes an object,) and start using "thou." In doing so, we have a whole new relationship — with everything. We become part of a web of action and response, of change and balance.

Our separation has been "manomaya" — mind-made, as Joanna Macy calls it. With the disappearance of separation, the ear opens to the possibility of a two way communication. This is usually the case in "relationship." There comes a time, says Vicki Noble, when you realize "something" is answering back, something is "talking" to you. That moment changes you forever.

These songs of the Navajo are both a singing of thanks and a desiring, a praying for balance, for healing of dis-ease within the house. The words, chanted or sung, are the vocal expression of the Navajo healing mandalas, paintings of sand. Within the circle, in ritual and symbol drawn, the person in sung (prayed) back into balance within the house of body, and within the house of living earth. Within both houses and between both houses must balance the elements of life — air, fire, water, matter.

This "mixing" of the elements creates growth and change. Inherent in the mixing is an impulse toward balance. In a Huichol yarn painting Grandmother Growth lies dreaming over a cauldron, the mixing pot of life. She holds in her hand a wand that contains her heart. From the prayers of her dreaming, from the wand of her heart, spirals growth. From her heart pours forth: the corn, the flowers, the eagle, the deer, and the snake — the salamanders and suns; the snakes and rains. From the heart flower of the center of this mandala all of creation grows in balance.

As the Navajo healing prayer comes to a close, an abundance, "pollen," falls all around: corn and plants, dews and rains, good relations with family, lovers, and friends; respect of elders, peers, and children — and you walk in beauty:

> *With beauty before me, I walk.*
> *With beauty behind me, I walk.*
> *With beauty below me, I walk.*
> *With beauty above me, I walk.*
> *With beauty all around me, I walk.*
> *It is finished (again) in beauty.*
> *It is finished in beauty.*
> *It is finished in beauty.*
> *It is finished in beauty.*[5]

Remembering "how" to pray means remembering an "innocence" of heart that simply desires healing, that desires beauty and balance. It also means suspending the mind aspect that says this is nonsense. At the same time, we do not control the whole household. Nor are we able to see very far.

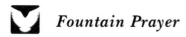 *Fountain Prayer*

A Journey of Imagination

(To do this journey, you need memory of "The Temple of the Soul" which you will find in the section Inhabiting Space.)

Find a safe and comfortable place. Breathe, release tension and ground. As you relax and focus inward, allow yourself to remember the music inside your soul temple. Let your awareness fill with this sound, feeling yourself once more inside that place of beauty. Dwell there, listening.

You begin to hear the waters of a fountain in the center of the temple. Feel the mists from its spray and see the rainbow light as its waters cascade into the air. Around the base are many stones of different sizes and shapes. Choose a stone that is your prayer stone. Hold the stone for a moment between your hands as you think or see what it is you desire. When the stone feels warm and "large" with your prayer, toss it into the fountain.

See the prayer rise in the rainbow light of the fountain mists. Feel the spray falling all around you. You may wish to offer more than one prayer. When you are finished, offer your thanks. Slowly breathe yourself back into present time.

 ## ON THE WINGS OF PRAYER

> *I circle around*
> *I circle around*
> *The boundaries of the earth*
> *The boundaries of the earth*
> *Wearing the long wing feathers I fly.*
>   excerpt from Arapaho Ghost Dance song[6]

Lifted on the wings of the Thunderbird, anything was possible. Anything could be transformed. So they danced, danced for the healing of the earth, danced for the healing of their people, danced into the beating of Thunderbird wings. In the winds, their prayers fly — that the earth be healed, that the people be healed. That the destruction stop.

Prayers fly from the heart. Propelled by desire, they are focused by intent. In many mythologies, prayer is carried on the wings of birds. Evelyn Eaton recalls the association of prayer and eagle: "the eagle's flight, because of its height and its swiftness stands for prayer rising to the Creator and grace descending to mortals."[7] The soft flutter of dove wings, on the other hand, may carry the yearning of the heart, the yearning that may not yet find even the words.

You may experience the flying of prayer as energy propelled "outward," flying until it reaches "its destination." You may actually feel the culmination of this outward flow, and then, a flow back to you. I call this cycle "arcing." It might also be called prayer and grace.

A woman spoke of playing the drum and of the moment when "a dolphin came" and took her hands — and she broke through the waters, surrendering to sound. And so it is, too, she said, with prayer. There is a place where outcome is surrendered.

 Bird Prayers

A Journey of Imagination

Find a safe and comfortable place. Breathe, release tension, and ground.

See yourself sitting in a special place upon the earth — perhaps a high mountain, or a desert, or a forest, or the ocean. You will know where. Let this place become larger in your awareness, breathing the smells, hearing the winds in the trees, the songs and the cries of birds in the distance.

Become aware of the prayer that you hold in your heart and the desire that stirs within you. With your heart, call for the help of a bird in prayer. Wait.

When you feel the bird's presence, release the prayer to the flight of wings. See it fly. You may give it voice in chant or song. When the prayer reaches its destination, allow the return flight to happen. Surrender your heart in thanks.

 SOUNDING A JOYFUL ECHO

> *The song resounds back from our Creator with joy.*
> *And we of the earth repeat it to our Creator.*
> *At the appearing of the yellow light,*
> *Repeats and repeats again the joyful echo,*
> *Sounds and resounds for times to come.*
> from *The Song of Creation, Book of the Hopi*[8]

There are only two necessary attitudes, says Shaman healer Vicki Noble: to give thanks and to pray. These two are inseparable from each other. To give thanks is to accept knowledge (acknowledge) our gifts. As we give thanks, celebrating the bountifulness of our lives, the heart opens and love flows back to the source.

The singing of thanks, we are told by the Hopi creation myth, "echoes" the sound of creation and is our life cord to source. Spider Woman took some earth, it is told, mixed it with saliva, and formed two beings. She covered them with her silvery cape, woven of the wisdom of creation, and sang to them the Creation Song. To one she gave the duty of form — to create order by solidifying creation. To the other, she gave the duty of sound — to create order by sending sound throughout the land. This one she called Echo, "for all sound echoes the creator." And so the first peoples were told to remember — to remember to sing their songs of thanks to the source from which all flowed.[9]

Giving thanks, says David Spangler, is an essential part of manifestation. If we forget to give thanks for what we receive, we are not likely to receive more, and, in fact, we may lose what we already have. Accumulation, houses and closets full of unused "things," weight us down and diminish our ability to attract the new, says Spangler.[10] Material possessions are energy in form. If they are not vital to our life, they need to be recycled and their energy released.

 Thank Full Page

1. Begin a thank full list

2. Write your songs of thanks. Give voice to your thanks by reading, speaking, singing, or simply humming your songs.

3. Using strips of sack paper and water proof ink or crayon create images of thanks. String them with yarn and hang them in your house or in your garden for the winds to catch.

4. Create a thank full garden or altar with stones, shells sticks, plants...that symbolize your thanks.

5. What gifts do others see in you or around you that you have trouble acknowledging? Name them. Give thanks for them.

6. Create a birthday ritual: To give thanks for the gifts of your life on your birthday is a sure way to receive the blessings of a happy birthday. Use any of the ways of thankfulness above or make it a special ritual that you share with those close to you. What are your gifts? Name them.

   You might include a naming mandala in your birthday ritual. Write your name in the center; radiating from the center, words or images that describe the qualities that mirror you and your aspirations for growth.

 ## SQUARING THE CIRCLE

There is one more essential law of manifestation: being willing to do the work that brings the dream into form. The "child" must be labored into birth. Rarely is this experience exactly what we expect.

One morning recently, I stood in the check-out line of a super market, feeling a bit scruffy from working on the land. "My fingers are getting fat from punching this computer," the man who was checking remarked. "Muscular," I said. "No, fat," he insisted. I prefer to see it as "muscular," I thought, looking at my worn hands. Scratched and scraped by the forest, toughened by cold and sun, dirt and concrete; they are working hands. There are times, when confronted by the manicured hands of a bank teller, for instance, that I am self conscious about them, and try to keep the fingernails out of sight.

Somehow I thought there would be more glamour — and, a little less work — when I dreamed the dream of Wanderland. I remember Thoreau's advice in *Walden:* you have dreamed your mansions in the sky, now put the foundations under them. The image definitely seemed more romantic than building the foundation of Wanderhouse.

"Humility," I discovered about half way through the project is related to "humus." That made sense to me as I worked on my hands and knees, cleaning the trenches for the foundation footing one more time. It should be as free of litter as possible for the concrete pouring, I was told. And then, the very hour that the concrete truck lumbered up our newly built road, the rains came, Two inches in four hours. The trenches became rivers; our boots made sucking noises in the muck as we slipped and sloshed, and sometimes fell into the morass of the house site. We worked on into the night, drenched, smeared with mud and concrete, moving slowly by the light of propane lanterns.

"What happened to your hands?" a student asked me the next day as I faced the florescent-lit reality of a composition class. Looking down, I saw how sore they were. It was the first I had noticed.

Hands move around the outer border of the spider mandala worn as a throat shield by Spiro women. In the center, the belly of Spider, spins a wheel of the four, the primal polarities. Out from this, Spider's eight legs tap and shape the web of creation. She is a creatress: a spinner, a weaver, and a cutter. And so are we, the mandala reminds us, our human hands shaping and creating — doing our work.

Work of The Hands

Preparation: For a day or more dwell with your hands. Notice what they enjoy doing. Do a mirror meditation with them, letting them move in any way that pleases you.

Create a "hand portrait," Use as many images of your hands as you like; let each of the hands express its work, what it wishes to create. The portrait could be imaged as a sequence on a cave wall or stone; it could take the shape of a mandala; or perhaps the design around a vessel or pot.

Journeying In The Realms of Down-under

Possibly the twelve had willingly given up their life forces to nourish the spark still flickering in the remaining, precious, youngest, thirteenth child...

ANN CAMERON, *Daughters of Copperwoman*

 ## MOON WISDOM

"Tell them," Moon said to grandmother Turtle, in a Native American teaching, "Tell them that as I in living die, so they, too, in dying shall live again." This is Moon's teaching night by night, month by month through the millennia from the moment so long ago when she first touched human imagination.

Our ancestors carved her form, as woman, at the entrance to a cave in Laussel, France, twenty-five thousand years ago. Her left hand holds the full curve of her belly. In her right hand, she holds a crescent shaped bison horn etched with thirteen lines, marking the monthly cycles of a lunar year. The animal's crescent horns, like the waxing and waning crescents of the moon, danced across cave walls, and in the night sky as she later became the wild Cow of Heaven (in Egypt, Hathor) spraying her starry milk in galaxies (galaktos/milk). Even now, looking up into the night sky, we speak of our own galactic home, spiraling around us as "The Milky Way."

Some say Moon is Earth's sister — born in the same moment of universal time. In her dance with sun and earth, she teaches us; again and again, with her own body she teaches us, the spiraling of change. "The spiral movement that creates a center and a moving, continuous whole is also that which, combined with gravitational contraction, creates the solar system, and the atom — and on a large scale, the galaxy."[1]

The spiral is imprinted close to home as well. We see it in the DNA, in a snail's shell, in a spider web, in the swirl of moving water. It is this repetition of a pattern on many levels at once, that makes mythology a holographic language. According to the dictionary, another meaning of holographic is "signed by the author."

Moon's spiral dance is also a dance of the waters, of the tides, of the rains, of the menstrual flow, of our emotions. Three-fourths of our bodies and three-fourths of earth body is water. Moon pulls the waters of growth. For millennia folk wisdom has told us that her light and her magnetism pull the new sprouts through the dark soil.

Moon, herself, is born again and again from the seed of darkness. And to this place of renewal, she dies again and again — shedding her silvery skins as she goes.

©1987 Winky Wheeler

Song To She Who Changes

Moon One
Dark One
Silver light
Shedding One

Moon One
Shining One
Waxing and
Waning One

Glowing One
Moon One
Growing One
Moon One

Cow of Heaven
Horns of Light

Lunar One
Moon One
Silver light
Shining One.

gwendolyn

 Old Skins

Moon, like snake, like us, renews herself by shedding old skins. What is no longer vital to growth, even though it may be beautiful, withers and dies as the new is born.

Sometimes old skins can be detected by major changes in your life style and clothing style. What old skins have you shed in your growing? What old skins are you now shedding?

Moving out from a center that represents your growing core, sketch these old skins. Are there any places where they still cling? Use color, texture, patterns, images to show how they feel and look to you now.

When The Ear Opens

In the myth of Inanna (Wolkstein and Kramer edition) the lovers sing the abundance of their pleasure in the sacred marriage scene. Their bodies, meeting, become a cornucopia of the earth's abundance — ripening fruit, fields full with grain, the store house filled with milk and honey. Then, abruptly, as the scene draws to a close, so, too, does the lovers' relationship. Inanna's songs become a lament: "Now, his sweet love is sated. Now he says: 'Set me free, my sister, set me free. You will be a little daughter to my father. Come, my beloved sister, I would go to the palace. Set me free...'"[2]

Many women hear this scene with a shock of recognition, so contemporary is the relationship dynamic. "First, he wants her; then he wants his space back; next he'll hit the road," they comment. One man explained to me that "after a man has an intimate experience, he needs some space. He needs to come back into himself." "I think," I replied, "that after a woman has an intimate experience, she most often feels even closer to her partner." All we understood in the moment was that we were discussing a male/female dilemma that was over 4,000 years old.

"My blossom bearer," sings Inanna as the two part, "your allure was sweet. Dumuzi-Abzu, your allure was sweet." Dumuzi's path moves outward: he is restless to use the powers of kingship he has received from the goddess. The sacred marriage was, we must remember, a cultural ritual in Sumeria, an initiation of the king to ensure his union with the goddess and the land. Only by this union would his rulership and the land prosper. At the same time, Dumuzi's dismissal of Inanna as his "sister," and "little daughter to my father" is not only a shift in the relationship, but a reflection of patriarchal Sumeria, where masculine holds more power and value than feminine.

Inanna, however, in her grieving, moves inward; she must attend a funeral she tells Neti, the gatekeeper of the Underworld. The Bull of Heaven, "her sister's husband" is dead. She can hear the moaning, the grieving deep down inside of her. And she listens.

From the Great Above she opened her ear
to the Great Below. From the Great Above
The Goddess opened her ear to the Great Below.
From the Great Above Inanna opened her ear to the Great Below.[3]

Inanna abandons Heaven and Earth to follow this inner call. She begins her descent to the Underworld.

On the wheel of change, the story has made a cyclic turn from the full bloom of summer into the dying back of fall. In the soul's journey of Inanna, the story shifts from outward expansion to inward integration. In the personal story, the loss of bliss, the death of a relationship, opens the ear to the Great Below. This kind of blow to the heart, whether through physical death or separation, is a frequent doorway to the Underworld. When it happens, what has previously nurtured us, given our lives meaning, given us identity and purpose comes to an end. We are sent down under to feel the grieving, to attend the funeral. We do not know, at the time, how long it will take before we hear the first birthing cries of our own return.

The ear that "opens" hears the soul's voice and brings us closer to the growing place. In Sumerian, the word for "ear" and "wisdom" is the same.[4] The water god, Enki, who is also god of wisdom, has a throne directly above the watery deep. His ears are "wide open" to the Underworld. Enki, like Odin, receives the gifts of feminine wisdom through an Underworld initiation — an initiation of death and rebirth. Perhaps it is because Odin is a sky god that he becomes "one-eyed," that bird-like, he sees with the eye of wisdom. Enki, however, is a water god who travels the changeable seas of emotion; his art is empathy. He listens. His ears are open.

Mythology tells us that there is not only a third-eye, but also a third-ear and that both are perceivers of wisdom. Clarissa Pinkola Estes has pointed out that ancient disectionists described the auditory nerve as having three pathways deep in the brain. They surmised from this that we were meant to hear at three different levels: one pathway was to hear mundane conversations of the world; a second, learning and art; and the third existed so "the soul itself might hear guidance and gain knowledge while here on earth."[5]

The call to go "down under" might come as restlessness, anxiety, boredom, depression; it might come through vision or dream; it might come by processing emotion or by a voice breaking through the surface of sleep. One might also be called through a sudden shock — an accident, a death, an ending. But once the call is heard, the descent begins. Spiraling down through the labyrinthian depths, we are pulled back to the vital core — to the dying/birthing place.

 Landscape of the Grand Round

Without analyzing or worrying about whether you know or don't know, sketch in the words, colors, images, you associate with each of the two realms.

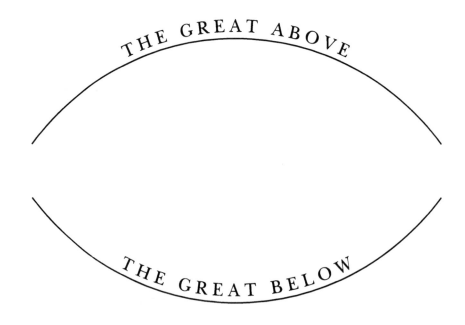

Landscape of the Two Realms

1. From your initial free association, create each realm as landscape. What is the terrain? (mountain, desert, sea... allow the possibility of landscapes you have never seen before.)

2. What is the weather?

3. Who are the animals and birds that inhabit each realm? (Again follow "first thought" without analysis)

4. Who are the goddesses and gods?

 Looking At The Polarities

1. The image a culture gives to The Great Below appears to be associated with the elements that cause the most change and destruction in that region: for example, floods, storms, heat, drought. People, as well, use elemental metaphors to describe their psychological and emotional experience of the Underworld — watery depths, waste land, gray fog, tempests, underground cavern. The dominant element of their landscape is often the transformational element they are working with in their own changing. For instance, water: the emotions; fire: passion, anger; air: thought-forms: earth: body, form.

    Look back at your landscape of The Great Below. What element (s) — earth, water, air, fire — is dominant in the landscape? Free associate around the element to see what meanings it has for you.

2. Most of us have received much conditioning that leads us to see The Great Above as good and The Great Below as bad. Look back at your two realms. What color typifies The Great Above for you? The Great Below? Free associate around that color. Notice to what extent you have created opposites of the two realms.

 The Magic Mountain

For a moment, imagine a beautiful mountain. Weather moves and changes around the mountain: clouds and mists and sun; lightning and thunder and tempestuous storms. It feels like the mountain has been here forever, so enormous and so ancient its form.

Every year the mountain blooms and changes as the seasons turn. The music of the mountains changing is in the winds and in the waters, in the trees, and in the songs of the animals and birds. The people, too, sing their songs to the mountain. They sing of the Magic Mountain, the mountain like the belly of The Mother, that holds a great mystery — the mystery of life, death, and rebirth.

The oldest stories say that the spirits of the dead return to the mountain where like seeds in the dark earth, they shed their form, giving life to the new. Paleolithic people buried their dead curled in fetal position and painted with red ochre. In this way, they returned them to the belly of the Mother, with the knowing that they would be born again.

Inside the mountain were the ancestral spirits of animals and people. Inside was the well of time beyond measure that some call Dream-Time — the realm of vision and dream, the spirit realm. It was natural for the living to journey into Dream-Time, to pass back and forth between the realms, for they were not separate. They would journey Down Under to hear the wisdom of the generations of time, to hear the voices of the ancestors. They would journey down to make their own passage, to die to their old self, for this was the place of transformation.

 Ancestral Mountain

1. Sketch the form of the mountain as you see it in your imagination. (colored chalk and black roofing paper works well)

2. Create the inside of the mountain.

3. Who are the ancestors that guide you? (these may be animal, plant, people) Sketch them in with images.

4. What lies for you in the mountain waiting to be reborn? Sketch in with images. (You may wish to glance back at your map of the Great Below to see what is there.)

 Making a Dreamscape

Draw the horizon — dividing upper and lower. You might wish to use a long piece of paper. Black roofing paper (light weight) and colored chalk work well for the project. Every morning for at least a week, spend a few moments sketching dream memories. You can do this with titles, words, images, colors, lines of force or flow. Know that you can add detail later if you like.

Some memories will be above the surface, or horizon, clear in your memory. Others, will be below the surface, "remembered" only as feeling or sensation. If no images surface, create the feeling of the sleep in color or image.

This project allows you to see your dreamscape from a distance and over a period of time. It also helps you dwell with dream images, allowing them to expand in your consciousness. Dreamscapes make powerful murals for your sleeping space or dream circle.

DREAM CATCHER

Silken I spin the net
Silken I weave the web

Dream Catcher
Spin from me

catch my self
speaking to me

Dream Catcher
Spin from me

reflect myself
seeing me —

Dream Catcher

spun in the seas
silken nets
attracting poss abilities

Dream Catcher
bring to me

be my fingers
reaching visions
be my fingers
touching clarity
be my flowering ears
under the seas

Dream Catcher
bring to me...
gwendolyn

Catching Dreams

Perhaps it was Grandmother Spider, with her silvery threads weaving a net between heaven and earth, who first taught people to make Dream Catchers. They can be made in many ways; the important element is to put into the creation your intent to "net" your dreams.

Using words, images, color, materials, create a net to catch your dreams. This may be done as song or poem, as a drawing, or more traditionally in the shape of a web, using a hoop and threads. Hang your dream catcher near your sleeping place.

JOURNEY DOWN UNDER

In Sumeria of about 2500 BCE, when the myth Inanna was recorded, the Underworld Mountain, called the Kur, had begun to take on some of the negative connotations later associated with the Christian hell. The word "hell" derives from the early metaphoric use of "hill" as the belly of the goddess but the later meaning focuses on judgment, punishment, and suffering instead of regeneration.

What makes the myth of Inanna so fascinating is that the vestiges of the old way of seeing are still present. The myth was recorded in the cultural time when both god and goddess were living archetypal images, but god, man, and heavens were beginning to sever from goddess, woman, and earth. The severing was accomplished by domination, repression, and violence.

Thus, in the myth, the king unites with the goddess, but also separates from the goddess and assumes a superior and self-important position, and the brother "helps" his sister with a 600 pound ax and armor heavy enough to shield any male heart from feeling. The wild maid, Lilith, is driven out and Inanna is "given" her throne and bed. Father Enki has possession of the "Holy Me" as well as the "Vessel of Urash" (Earth Vessel). And the Great Mother, Ereshkigal, whose name means Earth Vessel, is seen as a nasty, devouring, insatiable hag. In other words, patriarchy's image of a "witch." No one much likes her — besides, she's angry.

The story of Inanna had evolved for a long time before its recording. Inanna represents a very old archetype. As Queen of Heaven, she is the moon and represents the triune cycle of change. As Queen of Earth, she is both cornucopia of abundance and vessel of regeneration. In spite of the patriarchal overlay, the myth presents in clear outline the ancient archetypal pattern of the Grand Round, the Wheel of Change.

Four thousand years after the recording of this myth, many still find in Inanna's descent a mythic frame for their own underworld journeys, and most importantly, an archetype that shows the journey Down Under as part of the growing process. This is particularly important in a culture that has tended to label such experiences in negative ways: nervous breakdown, depression, middle-age crisis, neuroses. Inanna's experience of descent goes like this:

For a moment, it seems that she has most everything — so great is her fullness, so abundant is her life. She has status, power, beauty; she has a luxuriant home, a lover, children. People admire her. Then something goes wrong. She is not even sure what it was. Her lover leaves. Her heart hurts. The foundations of her life begin to crumble. She cannot ignore the pain inside her. She is grieving.

But she is still Inanna, Queen of Heaven and Earth. She will not let this get her down. She adorns herself in her finest clothes. She wears her Lapis beads. She carries the emblems of her Queenship. She holds the seven Holy Me in her hands (seven in Sumerian is the number of wholeness.) She has powerful medicine. She also has the good sense to enlist the help of an ally, Ninshubur, in case she doesn't come back.

When Inanna arrives at the outer gates to the Underworld, the gatekeeper, Neti, describes her as "tall as heaven, as wide as the earth, as strong as the foundations of the city." "Open the gates," Inanna demands, "I am Inanna, Queen of Heaven, on my way to the East." (On one level of the myth, she is the planet, Venus sailing beneath the horizon to rise again in the East.) "Why has your heart led you this way?" Neti asks. "Because the husband of my older sister is dead," Inanna replies. "I would attend his funeral."[6]

Ereshkigal, however, is not pleased with this sister who has come dressed in her finery and status. Her eyes flash, she bites her lip, and one can imagine gnashes her teeth as well. Who does Inanna think she is? If her life were that great, she wouldn't be coming down here.

"Allow her to enter," Ereshkigal says, "but strip her." At each of the seven gates, Inanna must surrender some part of herself. When she protests, she is told, "Be quiet, the ways of the Underworld are perfect." She is stripped — of her power, of her allure, of her identity, of all that had formed who she was. She stands naked and vulnerable before the eyes of Ereshkigal. There is no pretense. She stands before the eye of truth.

What is old must die to be reborn. Ereshkigal is the Earth, the great composter. She is the vessel of transformation. She is also "sister" of Inanna, a sister that was driven down a long time ago. Ereshkigal is the power — of goddess and of woman — that in the beginning of the myth is repressed. She is "given" the Underworld for her domain. She is an older, angrier, Lilith, who has been in exile now for a long time.

Ereshkigal is a vital part of Inanna, crying to be heard. And she is ready to strike down anything that is false. She pronounces Inanna's "guilt," and "fixes her with the eye of death." For three days, as the moon is in its dark, she is a corpse "hung on a peg" (like an old overcoat) in the Underworld.

In the Throne Room of the Underworld, Ereshkigal is "moaning with the cries of a woman about to give birth. No linen is spread over her body. Her breasts are uncovered. Her hair swirls about her head like leeks."[7]

"Oh my inside; oh my outside. Oh my inside; oh my outside," she moans. As the sliver of the crescent moon appears in the dark night sky on the fourth day — the god of the waters, Enki, sends the gifts of life: "the bread of life and the water of life" (body and blood). Inanna is born newly from the Great Below to the Great Above. Wearing her mantle of darkness, she walks toward the light. The wheel has turned.

 ## Gateways To The Underworld

What gateways have led you into the underworld? Sketch these, giving each a name and design.

Seven Gateways

There are seven gateways to the Underworld in Inanna's archetypal descent, from the first gateway where she surrenders her crown to the seventh where her royal robe is removed. For a moment assume a correspondence between these gateways and the seven gateways or chakras of your body. One person sketched the correspondence like this:

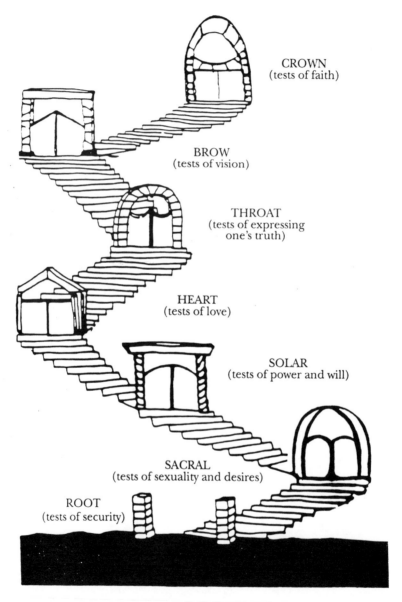

Journal sketch of the seven gateways seen as chakra initiations.

1. From your Gateways to the Underworld, choose one you wish to work with. It is important to remember when working with Underworld material that you always choose whether or not to open a door. Some remain closed because it would not serve your growth, at present, to open them again. Follow your feelings on this.

2. Draw the gateway, using images and design that evoke the kind of initiation it was for you. Which of the seven archetypal gateways does it correspond to? What did you sacrifice when you passed through?

3. Since our bodies are holographic, each chakra has not only its own identity, its particular vibration, but also the vibration of all the other chakras within it. In the same way, each gateway is the holograph of all the others. Hence, if you enter the Underworld through the gateway of the heart, as Inanna does, you may also experience initiations in security, in emotions, in power, in voice, and in mind. Sketch the succession of gateways you passed through. What was given up at each?

 ## OLD CRONE MOTHER

For weeks the Tarot had been telling me "Tower." It bounced all across the mandala layout I use. Tower in finances. Tower in the feminine. Tower in work. Tower in my own body. Unexpected bills came. Unexpected expenses came. Work plans changed abruptly. Social plans fell apart. A new relationship ended. "Death" said the Tarot "in relationship." "No kidding," I thought grimly. Not even that ending was of my choosing.

For weeks I had also been resisting the rewriting of Movement Six, The Journey Down Under. "It's not a good time. I don't want to go down," I rationalized. Then one sunny morning, Luna and I went for our morning walk, as we always do. Just a few paces from the house, I bent over to tie my moccasin, holding Luna's reel leash for a moment between my knees. Luna, however, kept going and the leash unexpectedly became a weapon with a blow to the chin that knocked me to the cement. My mouth was full of broken enamel. I couldn't believe the morning had changed so fast. I sat with an ice pack on my aching jaw, trying to keep my tongue off the two jaggedly broken teeth, and thought of a phrase from Robert Frost: how is it that "the first tool you step on" (for him it was a hoe) "becomes a weapon?"

"Tower" is when the familiar — what you have counted on, what has given you security — suddenly crumbles beneath you. I was beginning to surrender to it. "All right, all right, I'm already going down," I thought; "I guess there was no decision to make." But there were still more minor accidents: knocking myself out on a low beam of the foundation structure, breaking my little toe, a root beer spill that wiped out two full data disks of writing, breaking my tail light while backing into another car (I didn't seem to be seeing too clearly in reverse!) "Hanged One" said the Tarot. I surrendered to the currents, praying and letting go; at the same time, letting the pain in my body take me inward to heal.

Then one day as I worked in the forest, I realized I had been chanting a song beneath my breath for some time. It went something like this:

> Old Crone Mother
> give birth in me
> Old Crone Mother
> set me free
> Old Crone Mother
> give birth to me

I was startled by the oddness of this prayer that rose spontaneously from me. "What kind of birthing comes of the Old Crone Mother?" I wondered.

That night I dreamt of a child, a strange child the size of a baby, but fully grown. She was a Japanese woman in her forties with a face full of enormous sadness. Her hair was piled tight on her head. Behind her, I glimpsed a headline about rape or violation, but couldn't quite catch what it was. Feeling the pull of her sadness, I took this baby into my arms and held her against my body, rocking her, cradling her. At first she seemed to accept my nurturing. I could feel her close against me. Then abruptly she pulled away and lashed out: "You think you can heal me, not even Ann could heal me, and you…." I couldn't quite hear her. "What did you say?" I asked? "You smell," she answered. I was startled awake by the harshness of her answer. My face tickled. I touched my cheeks and found my face wet with tears.

She was a strange, inconsolable child, this "old" baby of sadness. Her face and her taunting still haunted me the next day as did her defiance at having been "found." I recognized "Ann" as the woman I was a few years ago, a woman with a comfortable middle class life, children, and an intimate relationship that filled her time. Ann was a beautiful, nurturing woman. And, of course, "she who smells" was this loner, this woman I am now, who lives in a shed and an attic and whose primary relationship is with the earth.

I was surprised to find such a disagreeable baby, one so attached to pain; yet, also relieved. At last, I had seen her face and recognized her. I was six when she was conceived, this forty seven year old child of sadness. My mother braided my hair and wound it around my head. My father was gone. I felt my mother's terror and heard her crying. I saw the War in headlines and did not understand. I only knew how alone I was and how much fear there was around me. I was ten when the atom bombs were dropped on Hiroshima and Nagasaki — old enough to feel the rending, too young to know the world was changed forever. I cannot say that I have healed her, this abandoned self of mine. I only know that she has been birthed from that place of pain so long ago.

Last night was a warm summer night in the city. The futon where I sleep is directly in front of the dormer window so that often I am brushed by breezes or washed by moonlight. Last night was a full moon night; in fact, a blue moon. Waking and sleeping, waking and sleeping, I drifted in and out of the moonlight. Towards early morning, I danced and sang a song from the dreaming into the waking. It was a song of the frog and went something like this: "Kachee, Kachee, Kachee — frog turns round and round in her body." Over and over I sang the chant, feeling the turning and moving within me. Until, I was awake and the song and movement still in me.

An inexplicable happiness filled me. A frog song. I was delighted by it. Living in a rainforest, I know the sound and the look of frogs — the plop of their sudden leap just ahead of my feet when I walk; the full body vibration of their evening songs; the teeming sacks of eggs floating on the mud bottom of the ponds.

But there was something else I half remembered. I found it in Barbara Walker's *Woman's Encyclopedia of Myths and Secrets.* Frogs were associated with the Crone, with Hecate. "Egypt's Hekat," says Walker "was Queen of the Heavenly Midwives. Egypt made the frog a symbol of the fetus." Hecate's amulet of the frog was inscribed with the words of rebirth magic: "I Am the Resurrection." In Roman mythology, the frog was sacred to Venus, of whom Hecate was the Crone aspect. The triple yoni of Venus is sometimes shown as a "fleur-de-lil composed of three frogs."[8]

Today there is a lightness, a thankfulness in me — although I dare not describe it too closely for my mind only partly understands and I do not know what will next unfold. Still, I feel cradled by this Old Crone Mother of mine, newly born and trusting of Her. From here I grow.

 ## *Crone/Child Dialogue*

Be sure you are in a safe and comfortable place. Breathe, ground, and release tension. Allow yourself to drift back through the years, back to a time when you played as a child in a familiar place. See yourself playing. Continue to observe this child, your younger self. Feel the love and care you have for this beautiful child.

Hear yourself speaking from your years of experience. What would you tell this child about living? What would you share with this child?

When you feel complete with this interaction, breathe your self back into present time. Freewrite what you experienced.

 ## CRONE SIGHT

The "evil eye," it was called. It was said that with a glance she turned men to stone. Her raging presense guards the entrance to ancient temples of the goddess. She knows the holy place. Snakes writhe from her hair. Her eye fixes you, sees through you. She sees the Truth. She burns through delusion and pretense. She is outraged by violation. She destroys, cuts through, ends.

In patriarchy it was said that "witches" and old "hags" had the "evil eye." Stories were told of the monstrous Medusa, evil, devouring — killed by the hero, Perseus. Barbara Walker reminds us that a "hag" was a holy woman. Hag was a cognate of Egyptian "heq"— a matriarchal ruler "who knew the words of power." In Greece, she was "Hecate"— goddess of the dark moon.[9] In Egypt, the All Seeing Eye belonged to Maat, Goddess of Truth. It is Maat who guides the soul boat through the Underworld waters. In hieroglyphics, the mother syllable "ma" is an eye.

In Sumeria, she is Ereishkigal, the crone aspect of Inanna. When Inanna ascends from the Underworld, she does not come up like Persephone as a crocus on the winds of spring. Instead, she returns as Hag. She returns with Ereshkigal's piercing eyes. By the big apple tree in Uruk, she sees her husband, Dumuzi. He is dressed in his "shining me-garments," sitting on his "magnificent throne." He makes no move to greet her; he shows no compassion. In that moment, she *sees* him. She sees his self importance; she sees that he has taken the power as his own, that he thinks he is the ruler of the land, of the people, of herself. She feels the fire rising in her. She chooses. She uses her power. Inanna "fastens on Dumuzi the eye of death." "Take him," she says. "Take Dumuzi."

I like to fantasize that some priestess of the goddess snuck this scene into the recorded myth. It is such a clear image of the imbalance of power that was happening in patriarchy. I imagine matrifocal cultures around the world would have loved this show-down scene between the goddess and the king. It has a catharsis to it similar to the scene in the film, "Thelma and Louise" where the two surprise a truck driver who has been harassing them by shooting holes in his tires. It is time that Dumuzi is "brought down a peg or two."

As Dumuzi begins his underworld descent, Inanna grieves. We do not see her sitting on her magnificent throne in her shining me-garments. We hear her lamenting throughout the city. She has ended the relationship. Still she grieves. There is nothing that says crone power is easy or without pain. There is only the knowing that this is what you have to do.

Years ago, I came across the statement that the goddess will ask you to give up what is most precious to you. "No way," I thought, "I will hang on to what is most precious." Then came the day I had to choose to end a relationship that was "most precious" to me. I did not make this choice because the love had died, but because I knew I could not be who I was becoming and stay in the relationship. I grieved for a long time, much longer than most could understand. In the grieving, came the torment: "did I make a mistake?" "should I have chosen another way?" Although the choice sent me down, on a long Underworld journey, I came back again and again to the knowing: I could not grow into who I was becoming had I not chosen to end the relationship. What the goddess had asked of me was the strength to choose my Self.

Crone Power

1. When have you suddenly "seen" in a totally new way?

2. When have you "fastened with the eye of death" — assumed the power of ending?

 *Dark Skin Goddess*

Medusa

> Dark skin goddess
> Snake skin goddess
> Who are you in me?
> Eyes of fire
> Raging Desire
> Who are you in me?
> She who rises
> Mouth a hissing flame —
> Are you in me?
> She who fixes with her eye
> She who sees with her fire
> Are you in me.
> > gwendolyn

Dwell with the refrain "Dark skin goddess, snake skin goddess — who are you in me?" Let the question drift out as you think it, sing it, write it.

Listen for what answers come. Let go of time on this: it may take minutes, hours, days, weeks.... Simply hear what comes through. Free write, collage, draw, mold, sculpt the "answers." Or you might make masks of the images. A title might be: "Faces of the Dark Goddess in Me."

 ## DOVE FEATHERS AND LILIES

At first, I was puzzled about what it was that drifted like silver mist across the raw earth of the septic site. Looking closer, I saw tiny silken feathers, everywhere. Dove feathers. I had forgotten about the doves. For a moment, the memory saddened me. Every August now, for four years, ever since I had inhabited this part of the forest, I had watched the doves.

They flew softly, in flocks, through the tree tops, circling. I loved listening to the sound of their wings in the leaves and the coohooing of their songs. Last year, they flew in the trees that until just a month ago had covered this spot. That was the sadness in the memory. I picked up some of the tiny feathers and held them in my hand. They are softer than anything I know.

I worried that the doves had come this year only to find their habitat gone. Then I heard their soft fluttering and their coohooing song. They were deep in the forest but still doing their circle dance, still dusting the earth with their down.

Dove is the bird of Aphrodite. Dove is the softness of the heart opening, the voice of lovers singing to each other. Dove is sexual ecstasy rising in silver tipped cresting waves. Dove flies as soul. Dove is the mother's song, like milk flowing from her silken breast. And it is as dove, in Gypsy lore, that souls of the dead flew in and out of the Magic Mountain.

Aphrodite was originally a triune goddess, complete as Virgin, Mother, Crone. She is associated with the star, Venus. Her lineage runs back through the Middle East: Ishtar, Inanna, Ashtoreth, and Astarte. Astarte was the "mother star" or "Queen of the Stars," Walker says. "She ruled all the spirits of the dead who lived in heaven wearing bodies of light, visible from earth as stars. She was the mother of all souls in heaven, the moon surrounded by her star children, to whom she gave their astral (starry bodies)."[10]

As Venus — morning star, evening star —Aphrodite unites the polarities. Within her, the two come together as one. Within her, the sacred marriage occurs. Because of this, the number frequently associated symbolically with Aphrodite is six, a number that is connected in root and meaning with sex. In Greek it is "hex," in Latin "sex," and it is cognate with Egyptian "sexen,"— to embrace, to copulate.

The symbol for this union is the six pointed star, created by two interlocking triangles. In India this is the Tantric symbol of the perpetual union between the feminine Shakti (downward pointing triangle) and the masculine Shiva (upward pointing triangle). This union sustained life in the universe. The hexagram created by the two interlocking triangles triples the sixes, 666: six equal triangles in a six pointed star around a six sided center.[11] This is the union of the triune goddess with the triune god, the union of masculine and feminine in all three aspects. It is wholeness of self.

The flower of Aphrodite is a six petaled lily, drawn geometrically by using each of six points as a fulcrum at sixty degree intervals. The lily design, the hexagram and its number, 666, once marked the House of the Goddess, the place of sacred sexuality. The priestesses who taught the art of deep sexual/spiritual union were called by names of respect and honor — Vestal Virgins, Horae, Veshya. The conquering cultures called them "prostitutes."

Knowing this, it is not surprising that many now associate the number 666 as well as the word "hex" and "hexagram" with evil rather than with the Star Mother, Aphrodite. The reason for this can be said simply: when one religion conquers another, the old images and the old ways are forbidden. They become evil. This inversion of meaning is particularly striking around the images of Goddess religions that once evoked the sacredness and the power of female sexuality.

Some months ago, I had a dream about the number 666. I was in what seemed like an underground motel, at least there were various rooms and all appeared to be occupied. I had a message I was supposed to deliver, but I wasn't sure of the room number, only that I had to take the message to "my parents." The passages were confusing. I was lost. I knocked on the wrong door, and a woman rushed out, flustered and guilty. She was over-dressed, like a prostitute. She drove off in an ornate Cadillac. Finally, I found the room. "My parents," an older couple, came rushing out together. They, too, left as if evicted by my knock. When I awoke, I was amazed that I still remembered the room number, 666.

The dream and its sexual connotations, especially with the number 666, left me puzzled, and set me searching for the archetypal meanings of the number. The old residents, I knew, had fled at my call. Their leaving had opened the doors to some subterranean rooms in me where old sexual attitudes and feelings were trapped. "Time for some new inhabitants," I mused. New archetypes. I had no idea, at the time, however, that my searching would find an ancient archetypal Mother in room 666.

Nor did I know last June as I carried my first lily crop, pot by pot, thirty budded lilies in all, inside the concrete foundation of the unframed house — and, hopefully, out of the path of slugs — that I had given the six petaled flowers of Aphrodite room in the foundation of Wander House. Now, on this August day, they bloom in flaming reds and oranges, in soft petaled pinks and whites — tiger lilies, Asian lilies, Oriental lilies. They remind me of a heritage that says the fire of life is sacred. Dove feathers and lilies — a lovely late-summer harvest at Wanderland.

 ## House of Sexuality

1. Who inhabits your house of sexuality? What people, what experiences formed the foundation for your attitudes about sexuality? Give these images that represent the imprint they left with you.

2. Following impulse, choose an abstract shape to represent your house. Place these images within it, letting each have space proportionate to the impact you still feel from it. Where does the foundation of your house of sexuality need replacing?

3. What "ghosts of lovers past" still linger in your house? What rooms do they occupy? How much space do they have?

4. Use a color to highlight how much space *you* occupy in your house of sexuality.

 ## Remodeling

Redesign your house of sexuality using archetypal images of polarity and union or creating your own. Follow impulse about color, size, and arrangement.

 ## A DEMON STORY

I recognized its pull, the way it took me, spiraling down as if I were caught by a whirlpool I could not resist. I was sick of it. I had been battling this one for a long time. And still it had me. Somewhere, recently, I had read the names of the primary "demonic powers": ignorance, jealousy, pride, lust, hatred. I knew the name of the one that now held me: jealousy. Its particular twist was "abandonment." I had done enough emotional work to know how far back it went and even the experiences that gave birth to it in that little girl so long ago. Still, it would not let me go, but waited for the new experience that stirred once more the misery, sucking me down with it.

It was a November morning, close to Thanksgiving, as gray as the feelings within me. I glanced through a newspaper, looking for — anything. The ad read: "This empathetic man can show you how to release the shadows that hold back your growth." Why not? I called. The "demonologist," however, was from another state and appointments were being made for the end of January, two months away.

Demons tend to move in cycles like everything else. When January arrived, I no longer felt the intensity of its presence. Still I knew from experience that it was just awaiting its next opportunity to rise once more. I kept my appointment. He was a gentle man, soft spoken, but assured. I told him a little about myself. "I have noticed there is often darkness around women on a goddess path," he observed. Before I could think of a response, he had began his reading. "Once I begin, please do not interrupt the flow," he said. "I will look layer after layer, more deeply into you, and describe what I see." I listened as he focused on the darkness he saw within me, a darkness he described to the very core, where a child sat, he said "with a demon face." For one hour I listened — although I began to pray. "Goddess, stay with me, do not leave me." Why I did not run from the room, I do not know.

Later, I tried to explain to him the violation I felt. "I cannot make you give up your demons," he said. "I can only show them to you." He suggested I buy his tape and practice the meditations on it daily.

For days his words churned the darkness within me. I could only feel the pain. Doubt. Disgust. Rage. Despair. Negativity. Hopelessness. I did not know how to cleanse the experience.

"I need help," I said to a friend who is a Reiki practitioner. Stretched out on the floor of her apartment, I asked only to surrender to the healing. As the energy and light moved through my body, it felt as though I were being brushed by wings. "In the dark, focus on the light," a voice spoke within me. "Wherever there is darkness, there is a seed of light. Focus on the light and watch its radiance grow." Wherever I looked into the darkness and pain of my body, I could see this seed of light. Sometimes it was only a pin point, but as I looked, it grew in radiance. I had been given a gift, one I continued to use as a meditation in the days that followed.

A few days after this healing, I drifted to consciousness one early morning with the most blissful dream experience. In the dream, a "chariot" drew near. I do not know how else to describe it. In it was a presence I could not see. But I could hear distinctly the voice: "Show me your face, your beautiful, beautiful face. Show me your face," the voice repeated, over and over. And with each request, I felt myself opening, blossoming with an inexplicable beauty, again and again, opening. Awaking, the energy of the dream stayed with me for many days. "Show me your face, your beautiful face." I felt bathed in its radiance. And gifted beyond my words to say — to once more feel the beauty within me.

Playing Polarities

This free association game helps you see the "other face" of your demon, its polar opposite. Discovering this often helps you see more clearly what the demon is teaching you. Letting another person or a small group mirror back to you is most effective because it gives you distance on the pattern, but you can also work alone. It is also interesting to first do the exercise alone and then see how another's response compares to yours.

Working with another:

1. Name the pattern (you don't have to describe it, just give it a name.)

2. The other person names "opposite" qualities while you listen.
   For example: "abandonment" — trust, belonging, enjoyment, security, abundance, wholeness, independence, strength...

3. When the free-associating is finished, tell the other what quality or qualities seemed "right" to you. You will know this not by thinking about it, but rather by how they feel to you.

4. Trade roles, free-associating with the other person's pattern.

By yourself:

1. Write out the name of a negative pattern that you know you still battle. What qualities are its opposites? Write whatever comes for about ten minutes.

2. Go back and highlight the word or words that feel "right" to you. Claim the positive quality by writing it out as a description of yourself.

 ## GOING THROUGH THE WINDOW OF WOUNDING

"Every wounding is a window opening to a new reality." I am not sure where I first heard this. There is even a part of me that rebels against its platitudinal flavor. It is too easy. Some things hurt too much. Still the thought runs through my mind as I sit listening to the story told to me by a beautiful young woman.

She has spent most of her life healing a deep wounding first suffered when she was too small to defend herself. As a young girl, she was physically and sexually abused — violated by a member of her own family. She experienced the violation, the fear, the pain, over and over. But she still lived, even grew.

The young woman still does the work of healing that child within her, the sorrow, grief, and rage that live in her woman's body. She probably will all her life. She tells me she works in a crisis clinic for women and on an abuse hot line. She wonders how she can help more. Sometimes she feels hopeless. There is so much to heal inside of herself and outside herself.

Still, she grows, feeling the beauty around her in people, in the forest, in the starry night, in her lover, in herself. She speaks of a gift she has been given, a gift of compassion. She says she could not know what it is like if she had not been there, if she had not experienced the wound herself. It is this understanding, this empathy, that moves her to do more, to find other ways to help herself and others heal.

It is not an easy story. It is not an easy task. I know that I would, if I could, erase this wounding. I do not want it to happen; I do not want it to exist. At the same time, I see the purity of her face as she speaks of the work she knows has been given to her.

 ### Looking Through the Window

In words or images look through the window of a wounding. What is the new reality you see there?

 ### Shit Happens

"Shit Happens," says a bumper sticker.

It just does. Sometimes it just plain hurts. Sometimes it just isn't fair. Sometimes, it just doesn't make sense. Sometimes it just isn't beautiful.

Create a composting field. Place within it what still feels like shit to you.

MOVEMENT 7

Keeping Step With Changing Woman

"Changing Woman is hard to see. The pockets of time She lives in are small and fleeting, and She is always moving. Sometimes She's beside you, sometimes She's underneath you, and sometimes She's inside your heart. Sometimes She's in yesterday, and sometimes She's a few minutes from now. Sometimes She is a Girl, other times Teenager. Sometimes She's big and strong. Other times Her hair is snow white and She walks with a turquoise cane."

CAROLYN MC VICKAR EDWARDS,
The Story Teller's Goddess

 ## CHANGING WOMAN

Years ago, at a time when I was beginning to open to a period of very rapid spiritual growth, I had a dream that still stays vivid in my imagination. A woman sits playing an organ in a church. She wears a simple black dress and her hair is carefully combed and stacked on her head. She is as composed as the music she plays. Suddenly, there is a flash of lightening through the windows high above her. She topples from the stool and at the same moment a whole chorus appears, stylized as if in mime, mouths open, frozen in one expression — astonishment.

This is the way rapid growth has sometimes felt to me. Struck by lightening. Toppled from my foundations. Those around me left bewildered. "Who is this woman?" they wonder. At times, I wonder, too.

Sometimes I think that balance is simply keeping step with Changing Woman. Not to say that has been *easy* for me. I am, after all, a Capricorn — and there is a certain four cornered groundedness about that. I like my "hoofs" to feel solid even if the slope is steep and the ground shifting beneath me. But She — she who grows and changes in me and all around me — She sometimes spins very fast. In fact She has no aversion to going back to chaos if that's what is needed. At those times, the harder I try to control, the faster my feet move to keep up — the more out of step I become. "Breathe and let go," I have to remind myself. Dancing with Changing Woman means surrendering to the movement.

Last night in my mythology class, a woman spoke of what it means "to surrender." In a class exercise, she had drawn the beautiful image of a snake bird goddess, arms raised like the wings of a powerful bird. "To surrender does not mean giving up," she said. "It does not mean collapsing. It means *standing up*." Then she stood as if brought to her feet by her own words, raising her arms in a single movement upward like a flower unfolding. For a moment, she became the image she had drawn — a woman rising in her power, surrendering to the currents of change.

In India, She is called Sarasavati. She who like the river flows. From Her comes creativity — art, dance, writing, weaving. Like the river, She is continually changing. I have seen Her dance in the eyes and words of my students. I have watched Her change them and change their lives. I have felt Her dance in me and know that, time and again, I will follow Her call. Still, She is not always easy. She is particularly hard on anything you think should stay the same or last forever, relationship, for instance. Perhaps this is why we build the structures around relationships with such solidity, reinforcing them with legal and moral codes, and our own conditioned expectations.

At the time I ended my marriage, I had no models of divorce. My parents were married fifty years; my grandparents, the same. Divorce was simply not a concept I held. I remember sneaking a book out of the library called *Creative Divorce*, guilty to be reading it, yet pulled by the possibility of release from the constriction I was feeling. I had lived and grown inside this relationship for sixteen years. The structures of our family shaped my life. I baked, sewed, canned, nurtured, tended, gardened, read, played. Cleaned and cleaned some more.I was Mrs. so and so (not my own name). I led Blue Bird and Camp Fire Girl groups, Cub Scouts and Boy Scouts. I worked on PTA committees and went door to door for charitable causes. All this was part of me.

It is hard to say exactly when change begins. Sometimes its first sign is simply restlessness or boredom. If the structures around growth are too tight to allow it to happen, the symptoms continue to grow stronger: dullness, lack of energy, disease, depression, nervous breakdown, emotional illness. In this relationship, I was slow to listen. Not only did the relationship fit the idea of "marriage" I had been given, but I cared about the people around me and the life I had created.

I began to suffer from feelings of claustrophobia and suffocation. My dreams were vivid during this time. In one, I dreamt I was nailed into a box, unable to breathe, desperate to get out. I awoke on another night, sick with fear and guilt from a simple dream image, one that I experienced in my whole body: I saw a perfectly formed begonia plant, covered with tiny pink blossoms planted in a clay pot. Suddenly it started growing very rapidly. Its shape changed. It was a wolf eel, destructive and devouring. I knew it was me. I awoke with a fear and repulsion so strong that I knew what it meant to have your "blood run cold." I was cold clear through the bones. "Is this what I am becoming?" I worried. "Is my changing destructive?"

My fear and guilt about growth was so strong that it took me two more years before I could take the step out of the marriage. And even then, it was very hard. It meant losing both a role and an identity. It meant breaking a family and raising three children alone with no security or full time job. And it meant being viewed as a failure by my parents and relatives. I remember one day near the end of the relationship when my husband looked at me in frustration and anger. "So is this who you have become?" he asked. In the midst of the pain and confusion, I stood for a moment in clarity: I knew that this *was* who I had become.

One evening, years later, I sat across from another man, one I loved deeply. We had fallen in love at first sight and had no doubt we would love each other forever. For eight years we had grown and changed together. We had spun about us the belief that we were "soulmates" — two who had become as one. For a long while, it seemed we had everything. We spent hours and days playing and loving and being together. Our home became like "a garden" of beauty and we, frequently, in "paradise." Looking back, I do not know exactly when the changing began to stir inside of me; I only know it grew stronger and stronger until the momentum of that unfolding became more powerful than anything else.

That evening, my partner and I sat in our beautiful candle-lit home and looked at each other, each feeling the tension, the pain. For a while, we talked, trying to understand the other, but very rapidly we fell through all the layers of difference to the very foundation: "You are my *wife*," he said in anger and frustration. "I am not your wife. I am a *Crone*," I replied, claiming myself, feeling the fire flash in my voice and eyes.

That moment was the easy part. It was simply Truth. Inevitability can, at such times, feel like an anesthetic. The surrender it brings is a letting go to larger cycles. "Destiny" some have called it. It is definitely Crone territory. In *Daughters of Copperwoman*, Ann Cameron describes the feeling: "It was Time," she says. "Time for movement, Time for change, Time for expansion, Time to do as the trees in their time, move the seeds on the wings of the wind."[1]

What followed, however, was not easy. It may have been Time, but I was not ready to give up the relationship. It had taken the Crone rising in me to see the need. But there was another woman, a lover, a woman who was left grieving. And she was furious. A familiar and loved part of me had died and now hung, like the corpse of Inanna, on a peg in the Underworld. I felt like I had been split in two. There were times in the years that followed when all I wanted was to go back, to find her again, to be once more in that candle-lit house — to forget about Changing Woman.

One dream, in particular, showed me how deeply divided I was at that time. The dream was so vivid, so close to reality that it seemed to take place on the edge of dreaming and waking consciousness. I was sleeping in the forest shed. Suddenly, I sat up in fright. A huge, red spider was crawling across the bed, coming directly for me. Without hesitation, I smashed the spider with my hand. Then in a panic, I realized its mate was sitting in the other corner, only a few feet away, surrounded by her eggs — and she was furious. I was sick with the mistake I had made. In the moment of realizing that she, too, was coming for me, I awoke. I was shaking and *wide* awake, but there were no spiders in the shed.

Somewhere in spider lore, I have heard that the female of certain species will kill her mate because the male spider consumes what is needed for the young. The instinct is to protect the vital source, to give energy to what is being born. This is also the instinct of the Crone aspect of self. In my dream, I felt as though I had both witnessed and participated in a primal battle. To strike out for my own survival was deeply rooted in instinct. Yet, in the dream, I was sick with emotion at my own action and at odds with myself. I knew she who sat in the opposite corner was my own fury at the "death" of my mate. At the same time, the dream showed me the "eggs" I sat upon. They were vividly glowing, vibrant, ready to hatch. I was reminded of the words of a healer I had consulted a few years earlier: "You are sitting on an enormous amount of creativity, " he had said. "I think of myself as a creative person," I had replied. "Not compared to what you give up, and to what you stifle by busyness, by keeping things in order," he insisted. "No way," I thought at the time.

A central theme of Lynn Andrew's book, *Medicine Woman*, is the theft of the marriage basket. In the story, the basket is both a sacred artifact of Native People and a powerful symbol. As the story evolves, the basket takes on meanings of the womb, the physical vessel of creativity, and, at the same time, of woman's creative power. Many women are deeply moved by Andrew's story. They recognize in it, the patriarchal usurpation of feminine power, and, more personally, their own loss of power. In the story, the Medicine Man, Red Dog, has an hypnotic magnetism, an ability to "capture" the soul essence of women. At the same time, Lynn has an almost irresistible desire to merge with him, to give herself up. In the "battle scene" between the two, Lynn must cut through the maze of ethereal threads that entangle her with Red Dog to regain the marriage basket. Only by regaining possession of her own creative source does she make herself whole.

In those times of greatest change in my life, I have experienced what I call "a pendulum swing"— an opposite. Thus, what lies dormant, or is undeveloped, begins to grow. When this last relationship ended, I had been in couple relationships for over thirty years. During those years, I had defined my life by my partnership with another. I was now entering a time when my work was to give birth to what was "hatching" within me, a time when I would be tested and strengthened by walking alone.

 ## Pendulum Swings

Describe or draw the pendulum swings of your life (times when some part of your life changed radically). Pendulum swings in relationship, in work, in beliefs, in habitat, in life style.... Name the gifts you were given by each of the polarities.

 ## Judges of Change

In times of radical change who were your most severe judges? (Be open to the possibility that they were inside you as well as outside.) What was their verdict? Who did they want you to be?

 ## Tapestry of Change

Using a large sheet of paper, color or paint change as you have experienced it in your life. Use movement and pattern, texture and color to evoke the Changing One in you.

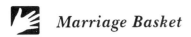
Marriage Basket

Draw, collage, or create a marriage basket, using colors and images that reflect the creative potential within you.

☙☙☙☙☙☙☙☙☙☙☙☙☙☙☙☙

STANDING BY YOUR WOMAN

Browsing the aisles of a bookstore recently, I noticed the lead article of a weekly newspaper: "Stand by Your Man," it proclaimed. I felt a vague guilt. It's an ethic some would say I have failed. "Maybe it's satiric," I thought. But I couldn't reach for the paper to find out.

In the heterosexual community, this unconditional support of a woman for "her man" is a code that has been around for a long time. It is an ethic that many think supercedes everything else, including the needs of the woman. The last several days, I have had the headline floating around in my head — with a slight reversal — just to see how it feels: "Stand by Your Woman." I think of my students' outrage when Inanna topples Dumuzi from the throne, where he sits superior, oblivious of her pain. "How could she *do* that to her husband?" they ask. "She is standing by her woman," I reply in my mind. I remember the disapproval of friends when I ended a relationship that no longer nurtured my growing self. "I am standing by my woman," I say. I try hearing a lover say to me: "I am standing by you while you grow; I know you are your own." It feels good. I am standing by my woman.

In fact, the force with which the Crone and Wild Woman archetypes are re-emerging shows that quite a few are "standing by their woman" with a fierce dedication to their own growth. Women are often fascinated to discover, for instance, that Eve has a rebellious "sister," one that has been in exile for a long time. The amount written about the archetype of Lilith in the last decade indicates how hungry women are for this dimension of themselves.

The name "Lilith" comes from "lily," forms of which were early names of the goddess. As flower of the goddess, she has to do with sexuality, with vital force — in other words, creative energy. From wild tiger lily to lotus blossom, from lotus blossom to tiger lily, she changes. In the heat of desire, in the ecstasy of opening, she grows. She feels the force of her own will. She resists what contains her. She leaps toward freedom. Her raging fires burn and consume what is in the way of her expression. She says "NO." She says "YES." She says "I want" and "I won't."

Lilith can slam out of the house and not come back. She can throw dishes at the wall and not clean up the mess. She can become an uncontrollable teenager — or an angry, sullen housewife. In the past, women have called her a "bad girl." She is not nice enough. She is not nurturing enough. Men say she seduces them and leaves them with no power.

In mythology we first meet her in Sumeria about 4500 years ago. She is driven, shrieking, from the tree of life that grows in the maid Inanna's holy garden. The scene mirrors back to us the "mythic moment" when the feminine was split by patriarchy. The wild forces of nature, the wild forces of the goddess, the wild forces within woman, herself, are "tamed." The powerful inhabitants of Inanna's tree — the snake, the Anzu bird, and Lilith — are driven from the tree of life. The tree is shaped into a throne and bed, and Inanna is "civilized" with the "help" of the warrior, Gilgamesh. The throne retains, for a while, connotations of the goddess: it is Her lap and the king's connection to her. But rapidly it becomes simply the king's throne, symbol of his power. The bed, at first, still symbolizes heiros gamos, the union of masculine and feminine. But in the evolution of mythology and culture, the Priestess of the sexual fires soon becomes "prostitute." Like Lilith, she is a bad girl. The one left, after the splitting of Inanna's tree, is the archetype we know as "Eve."

In Hebrew folklore Lilith is Adam's first wife — a job destined for failure. Female and male; male and female — they were, after all, created at the same time. When she cannot do what Adam desires (that she lay on the bottom in their coupling) she says NO and flies off to the Red Sea where she is viewed as demonic — seducer of men, killer of babies. She becomes woman's shadow side: she is not nurturing. It was then that Eve was created from the rib of man as wife of Adam. Perhaps it was then that she was taught to stand by her man.

As feminine polarities, Eve is deeply committed to relationship and to nurturing, whereas Lilith chooses self, again and again. Eve can give up too much of herself, live her life through the accomplishments of those around her, and lose her creative fire in the tidiness of keeping things under control. Lilith, on the other hand, is more likely to get out than to work it out. She is self absorbed, will stand by her woman, and is not good at staying in "her place." In a retelling of the story of Eve and Lilith, story teller Lynne Gottlieb, speaks of how these two polarities balance each other: "Eve means Life Bearing Woman; Lilith means Fiery Night Woman. And they are one and the same woman."[2]

Although the name Eve means Mother of All (The Goddess) and the name Adam means "born of the Red Earth," in the Genesis II version of creation, Eve is secondary and subordinate to Adam. She is born of man to be his companion and to bear his children. In this Biblical story, however, the Lilith fires are still not dead. In Eve's curiosity — her desire for pleasure, for knowing, for life — she reaches for the apple and tastes. She is disobedient. She does not stay in her place. She crosses the threshold and knows the secret of snake, the secret of moon. She knows of birthing and dying and birthing again. She knows the shedding of skins. She knows Changing Woman.

Lilith as Mirror of Self

For a glimpse of how expressed or repressed Lilith energy is in you, try quick responses to the following:

> times when you walked out
> times when you wish you had walked out
>
> times you said "no"
> times you wish you had said "no"
>
> times you broke the rules
> times you were a bad....
>
> times you went into "exile"
>
> times you did something wild

How alive is Lilith in your life right now?
What parts of you are in "exile"?

DON'T BOTHER ME LILITH, I'M BUSY

Like Inanna, many women experience the exile of their Lilith when they enter socialized womanhood, and like Inanna, many must go down to meet this fiery energy later in their lives. Often they are surprised at the intensity of its need for expression

In this dialogue, Karen Lowrie depicts the conflict that sometimes happens between the Eve and the Lilith aspects of self:

> "Eve, would you get *on* with it? Fuss, fuss, fuss — my God!
> How long will you keep me here pacing back and forth? Don't you try to turn me into some Goody-two Shoes, Suzie Homemaker twin, huhuh, oh no."
> "Hey in there, will you pipe down? There's just so much to do right now. Christine needs her hair braided. Theresa has a music lesson in half an hour. Michael needs to be picked up at ball practice and Baby Becky needs changing. Wait. Okay? I'm Busy. I've got this job to do — understand?"
> *"No, not really!* Things were just beginning to get exciting — 16, 17, 18 year olds — ahh well.... Boys, but with potential. And you, my sweety, becoming stronger, so much more independent. A blossoming flower sounds a bit corny but *we* know what I really mean don't we Eve-Karen?"
> "Hush, stop those thoughts, Lilith. You amaze me. How can you be part of me? Good grief! You are downright raunchy! I've just been elected co-chairman of our church school. This is not a time or place for you — go *away*."
> "Ohh Eve...?"
> "Hummm-m? Oh, it's you. Go *away*. I'm tired. If it's not babies keeping me

up all night, it's teenagers. I don't need you in my life now."

"*What!* I've been here all along you pea brain! Come-*on*, there's a few good sparks in you yet — wake up to the sensation woman!"

"Hum-m? No, no, not now…. And get out of my dreams, will you? Half the time I wake up in a cold sweat — stop laughing. You've proven your point, Lilith. With the graphic remembering of my teenage dates — oh dear, four teenagers — will I make it?"

"Ha! at the speed you're going, Eve, you'll run out of fuel before 40! Sometimes I wonder if you're worth the trouble. I'll hang on a bit longer. Hate to lose you completely."

"Lilith? Lilith? Are you there? God it's dark in here. I'm ready. Me, Karen, not Eve, but me. The kids are gone, the main part of my job is over. But I feel the spark of life. Lilith, I remember the feelings, the things you said…. I'm still young, well, sort of. I know there's life in me still. Are you there? Lilith?

"Oh my, ah yes — there you are Lilith. Must you do that? Oh, large aren't you? Is all that roaring, belching fire and smoke really necessary…?"

 ## Reunion

Invite your Eve and your Lilith to a reunion. Let them decide where they want to meet and what they want to do together to get re-acquainted.

Describe their interaction.

 ## WARRIORESS

It is Ninshubur who, in the myth, Inanna, stands by her woman. On the literal level of the myth, she is called a "sukkal," which is translated as servant. She serves Inanna well. It is she who meets and turns back the force of the warring water god, Enki. She is, in fact, an elemental polarity to Enki as East is to West, air to water, mind to emotion. Enki is changeable, emotional, tricky; Ninshubur is constant, clear, focused.

Ninshubur is described as Queen of the East. "Water has never touched her feet,"[3] we are told. As the part of self that transcends emotion, she is Inanna's life-line out of the Underworld. She also balances the sensuous, fiery, often tempestuous, Inanna.

In the myth, Ninshubur is a warrioress, because conflict and war were a reality in Sumeria of 2500 BCE. When conflict is not the reality, perhaps she will become a guide, for she is wise as well as strong. Ninshubur does not carry an ax or a sword. Hers is the force of will and intention. Facing the onslaught of Enki's power, "She sliced the air with her hand. She uttered an earth shattering cry."[4]

Ninshubur does not forsake her friend. It is she who gives strength as you stand firm for your truth. It is she who rises above the battle and gives focus to your intention.

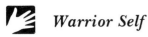

Warrior Self

Sketch with words or image:

What colors does your warrior-self wear? What elements do you associate with her? What animal powers does she have? What are her powers? What are her weapons?

Lake of Milk

A Journey of Imagination

"You are reminded that you must draw from the well to nourish and give to yourself. Then there will be more than enough to nourish others."[5]

From the *Rune Ansuz,* "Signals"

Stories about the Tree of Life, sometimes describe a "lake of milk" deep in its roots, at the center of the earth — at the heart of the Mother. This is the wellspring of inexhaustible nurturing. This journey of imagination takes you to this place through the pathway of yourself.

Find a comfortable place to sit where you will be uninterrupted. Begin conscious breathing to let go of the tension in your body. As you inhale, feel the light flowing down through your body into the earth. Breathing in the light; breathing out the light. Continue this process, feeling the flow of energy through you and into the earth. With each exhale, follow the energy down more and more deeply, feeling the warmth that surrounds you.

Breathing in, breathing out, letting yourself go, as if you are now sliding, down, down — until you break through, splashing into a lake of milk. Allow yourself to float in the radiance and warmth, feeling it wash through you, relaxing, filling every part of you. Spend as long as you like floating, playing, in this place.

When you are ready, when you feel so full that you desire no more, allow yourself to drift back up through your roots: on the inhale, the energy moving up through your body; on the exhale, the radiance washing over you like a fountain.

Continue this breath for a few more minutes, feeling your connection to the inexhaustible wellspring at the heart of the Mother.

SPIRALING THE POLAR DANCE

It is the third week in September, two nights before the Autumn Equinox. The night is clear and still, and full of stars. I walk the beach at Hug Point looking into the night sky. Wherever I look, more and more stars appear. I feel like I am falling into the sky, into the spiraling Milky Way.

Stars surround me. They are beneath my feet, reflected in tidal pools and in the sheen of the wet sand. I walk an invisible horizon between starry sky and starry earth.

There is a big cave on Hug Point beach that spirals inward like a sea shell. If you walk to its center, an eye of light suddenly appears, a window out to the moonlit ocean. But in its inner curves, it is blacker than night and you surrender your eyes, feeling your way along the cold, rocky walls. Tonight, I find a place to sit along the inner curve, breathing deeply the undersea smell. I sit silent for a long time looking into the darkness. The darkness becomes all, except for the sound of Luna's jingling tags as she circles outside the cave in the moonlight.

At Wanderland, the alder leaves are already falling and the earth's breath is cold even on a sunny morning. I am planting daffodils along the entry road. Fifty pounds of daffodils, a sack so heavy with gold I cannot carry it. Wheelbarrowing dirt, carrying buckets and buckets of daffodils, I play with a variation of one of Lloyd Reynold's Weathergrams. It is one I have loved for years:

> *Sunlight*
> *under dark soil*
> *comes up*
> *dandelion*

Only today, it is "daffodil." My hands are covered with dirt and full of sunlight.

For a brief moment, on these cool autumn days at Wanderland, I feel the balance of night and day, of dark and light. I have no doubt, however, watching the green go back to earth, that the momentum is toward the night. It will be a long spiraling in before the turning back toward light. Changing Woman dances this turning. She dances the balance of dark and light. Looking into the night sky, some saw Her starry body in the constellation, Ursa Major — The Great She Bear. They watched Her dance around the World Tree or Axis Mundi, whose tip was marked by the Pole Star. Her tail pointing to the east at nightfall told them of the coming of spring; to the south, the coming of summer; to the west, the coming of fall; and to the north, the coming of winter.

Our ancestors, many millennia ago, gave this dance the image of the rising and descending spiral, representing the constant double motion of the universe: in-breath/out-breath, in-tide/out-tide, fall-winter/spring-summer, waning moon/waxing moon.

The double spiral might be described this way: to the right — the spiraling out, the emergence, the creation, the bringing into form; to the left — the spiraling in, the re-emergence, the integration, the letting go. Drawn on cave walls, etched on stones, doodled on the note pads of school children, these spirals are part of our earliest symbolic language and reflect an ancient knowing — that the balance is in the rhythm of the dance. Sometimes they are the goddesses' breasts. Both outflow and inflow nurture us. Sometimes they are the goddesses' eyes. She sees with polar vision; She sees life and death as a spiral of change.

The double spiral sugests the balance of opposing vortical energies.
Through this balance wholeness is reached. (1240 BCE, Tarxien, Malta)

 Spiraling

1. First start with an exercise so you can feel the movement in your body. Move your hand in a circular motion, letting your arm take it — first to the left, circle on circle until you feel the energy flow; circle on circle, letting go. Do this until you feel the movement all the way up your arm. Repeat to the right: circle the hand, circle the hand, bringing in, bringing in, letting the feeling include the arm.

2. Now try both hands at once, going opposite directions.

3. Play with spiraling on the page. Make spirals and spirals, feeling the flow. Wait for impulse to tell you when to shift direction.

4. Notice what you are spiraling out and what you are spiraling in. Draw, color, or write what's flowing out; what's flowing in.

5. Play polarities: Allow yourself to swing back and forth on the page between what's coming in (writing time) and what's going out (social time). Notice that these are not necessarily positive/negative.

TRUSTING THE LIMITS OF CHANGE

As you played with spiraling, you may have found the outflowing and inflowing spirals joining. The two joined form the image of "infinity" — continuous, ever-changing movement. This image looks like an eight, lying on its side. The number  eight is about balance, the polarities joined with equal weight. In the traditional tarot, eight is called Justice, and the image is the scales, the two sides "weighing' against each other, balanced by a central pole.

Take a moment to explore the movement of the double spiral again, either on paper or by moving your arm in the eight of infinity. Notice that when the flow to the right has reached its fullness, the pull is back towards center; when the flow to the left has reached its fullness, the pull is back toward center.

The movement is similar to that of the Yin/Yang symbol with its two fishes of dark and light swimming the river of change. In this symbol, the eye of the fish represents the impulse back towards center. Hence, when the dark reaches its fullness (winter or night are examples in the physical world) then the light begins to grow in the eye of the fish and the journey is toward light. When the light reaches its fullness (summer or day) then the dark begins to grow in the eye of the fish and the journey is again toward darkness.

This cyclic turning is the dance of sun, moon, stars, planets, seasons, and, of course, our own growing. There comes a time, for instance, when the grieving falls away and life begins to stir in us again. There comes a time when we tire of social life and yearn inward toward solitude. And a time when inner work must be expressed in outer actions. If we are listening, we move back toward balance. If not, we experience dis/ease. Disease speaks the message more loudly — back toward balance, back toward balance.

Archetypally, the eight, especially the eight on its side without an upper or lower position, shows the equality of polarities — of solar and lunar, of masculine and feminine. Artist Sheila Broun has illustrated the cyclic movement created by polarities in her mandala of the wheel of change. The wheel turns in our inner cycles as in the earth's cycles.

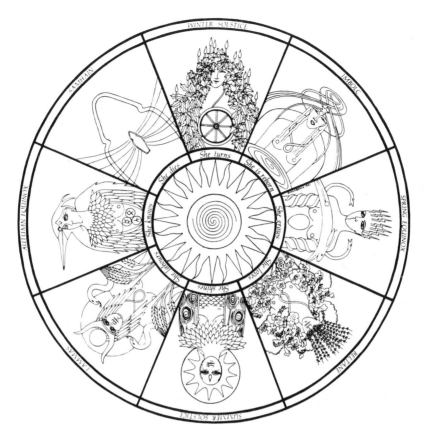

Goddess of the Wheel of the Year
Sheila Broun's mandala of change illustrates the
correspondence between inner and outer cycles.

 ## *Playing the Wheel*

1. Where is the earth right now in its cycle of change? Using Broun's mandala, where are you right now in your cycle of change? To what extent are you in synchronicity or opposition to the earth's cycle? (This is not "good or bad"; some people tend to be pulled by the earth's cycle; others not.)

2. What are you moving into on this wheel of change?

3. What is opposite of you? Write these oppositions at different ends of a sheet of paper and, in between, write words that describe your feeling about the tension between them. Or use color to express this polar tension.

4. See how it feels to join the two with an infinity spiral. As you spiral to each direction, feel the fullness of that polarity and the turning back toward center.

THE SCALES OF MAAT

I have loved the knowing, since I first came across it, that the oldest meaning of Truth is Balance — and that it is called by the name of Earth: Maat, matter, mother. Our ancestors knew that in her cycles and systems, Earth teaches us of balance in change. In Egyptian mythology, "seeing" this balance was the basis of wisdom. The mother syllable "ma" meant "to see"; in hieroglyphics, it was an eye."[6]

I fell in love with the Egyptian face of Maat the first time I saw Her. She is beautiful, sensuous and dark eyed — so beautiful she could be a young dancing woman caught in a moment of perfect balance, her hair a cloak of black, her face in golden radiance. It is Her eye, however, that magnetizes, that pulls you in, like falling into the night sky.

But do not mistake her intent. She is both your mirror and your guide. In Her, you are both "seen" and "seeing." In Egyptian hieroglyphics, She sits at the prow of your soul boat, her vision guiding you through the dark underworld waters, then birthing you into light as Metit, the Morning Boat of the Sun, the Mother of Dawn. In Her hand She holds the Ankh, the "key" of life. It is formed by the union of polarities: the cross and the circle. She does not promise that there will be no darkness. She provides the vision to "see" while traveling through the darkness.

The Egyptians say that Maat is guardian at the Gateway of Death. She is exact — Her scale so sensitive that it is balanced by an ostrich feather. It is against the feather of the Goddess of Truth that you must weigh your heart. A heart "as light as a feather" enters paradise.

In this imagery, Maat not only represents conscience (or judge) She also embodies law (or ethic). The foundation of Her law is balance, the balance inherent in the cycles and eco-systems of the Earth. An Egyptian, following The Code of Maat, was expected to walk lightly and to walk in balance with Earth, animals, people, and self; so that standing in Her presence at the Gateway, they could say of their life:

I have not been a person of anger.
I have done no evil to others.
I have not inflicted pain.
I have made none to weep.
I have done violence to no one.
I have not done harm unto animals.
I have not behaved with insolence
I have not judged hastily
I have not stirred up strife.
I have not insisted that excessive work be done for me.
I have not borne false witness…
from The Code of Maat.[7]

This code of the Egyptians, which is at least 4,000 years old, is a solid foundation for peaceful co-existence between people, the earth, and other beings. A similar ethical foundation has re-emerged in an agricultural philosophy called permaculture. Bill Mollison, author of the definitive text, *Permaculture: A Practical Guide for a Sustainable Future,* says that the ecological crisis is a failure of *vision*. If we recommit ourselves to thoughtful observation of the patterns in nature, Mollison suggests, "we will discover ways to work with nature to which we might otherwise be blind. There is only one ethical decision," says Mollison, and that is "to take responsibility for our own existence and that of our children."[8]

Maat (Mayet)
Egyptian Goddess of Truth and Justice personifies Divine Order

Clarifying Action

Write a code that clarifies your relationship with earth, people, animals, and plants.

 Short of the Mark

A man once explained to me that he had grown up in a Jewish tradition where sin and guilt were not stressed. If you made a mistake, you had simply "fallen short of the mark." This way of seeing gave him an optimism about his ability to grow and a more forgiving attitude toward himself and others.

1. Make a list of the times you think you fell short of the mark.

2. What *was* "the mark"? That is, what was your aspiration? What did you value?

3. Make a list of the times you felt others fell short of the mark.

4. What had you expected in their actions?

5. From this brainstorming, create a code of what you value in your own action and that of others.

 Aspiration

1. Create a symbol, or perhaps a landscape, that represents "the mark;" that is, your aspiration, what you are trying for in a particular situation.

2. Imagine that there is a pathway to this goal. Following first impulse, draw the pathway.

3. Where are you on the pathway?

4. What are the initiations on this path? Create them as gateways.

5. What stories do you tell of this journey? Give them titles. Which would you use as teaching stories for the youngers?

ONE DAY I DISCOVERED I WAS A FARMER

I have become a farmer. My grandfather would be pleased. He was a "first farmer" in the McKenzie River valley. He burned, sometimes dynamited, the enormous old growth stumps that covered the land so that he could plant orchards, and grow sorghum. As a child, I played, and worked with him in the lush peach orchards that by then had grown to full maturity on his land. The smell, the sight, the touch of peaches still brings those days to me. No peach, however, will ever match the taste of those red golden peaches in my grandfather's orchard that fell in my hand, heavy with ripeness.

This relationship with a place was a primary gift of my childhood. I spent summers playing in creeks and cotton wood river bottoms. I knew the river and its smell and how to catch fish and skip rocks. Weeding sorghum rows in the hot summer afternoons, I knew the feel of earth on my hands and against my knees. I have heard in folk wisdom that the gifts of your childhood, those things you loved most, will come back to you in old age. I often think of this when I walk Wanderland for I am still so amazed that I live in the midst of all this beauty. Once more, fifty years later, I have a relationship with a place.

Wanderland is a living rainforest, a small island on the slopes of a mostly clearcut mountain range, three miles from the Oregon coast. Sometimes people ask me if I own this land. It is hard to know how to answer; the word "own" is so totally inadequate in describing the kind of relationship this is for me. My father jokes that the land owns me. This is certainly true in work and attitude. When I fell in love with Wanderland, I was committed. There was no doubt this was a primary relationship, and as happens with any primary relationship, my life changed. The questions now were: How can I take care of this place and still take care of myself? How can I keep it from being destroyed without destroying it?

The answer to these questions has brought me back around to my childhood work, farming. It is a little surprising, even to me; but I like it. I would only modify the title in a few ways. I am a gardener as well as a farmer. I care for this place. I cultivate its growth, and love its beauty. I plant small gardens within the larger garden of the forest. I walk, I listen, and I observe. And the forest teaches me not only about a rainforest but also about myself.

As the farm at Wanderland grows into a business, I sometimes feel myself weighed against the feather of Maat. Do I have the right to change any part of this place? I was in the midst of this struggle with conscience while putting together the packaging logo and letterhead for the forest farm business. I had decided to use a simple image of a small seedling cupped in a human hand and had spent several hours working on size and placement of the image when I glanced at a book lying on my desk. It was Bill Mollison's book on permaculture. On the cover was a seedling carefully cupped in human hands.

I knew this was the attitude I wished to have toward farming at Wanderland. I now had a symbol for the "front door" of my new business. I also had a foundation, an ancestor root that extended back through my grandfather, but came with a new name: permaculture. These are some of the guidelines I wrote as I thought about how I wished to be in relationship with the land I farm: relocate plants from around the sides of the road and from areas cleared for building sites; grow seedlings in cleared areas; cultivate plants native to the forest and to particular niches in the forest; transplant from areas where plants are growing in profusion; care for and present plants to others in ways that acknowledge their beauty and value.

I want this forest to be here for a long, long time — until the Earth, herself, shifts and changes. I want the farming at Wanderland to help the forest speak of how valuable a living forest is — as a forest not a clear-cut. I want her to speak loudly enough so that the last 50 acres of 800 owned by the state on this mountain may also become a forest farm instead of a clearcut. I want my children to know forests — and their children's children's children…. This is my code, my foundation, as I become a farmer and a gardener of Wanderland.

 ## *Clarifying Foundations*

Write a code that forms a foundation for your relationship with your work.

 # HER NAME WAS MOON

In the beginning, the Creator does not speak directly to the people, according to the Pawnee. Tirawa, the One Above, sent certain animals to tell the people that he showed himself through the beasts, and that "from them, and from the stars and the sun and the moon, people should learn."[9] Tirawa, it was said, taught the people through his works. This primary intelligence in creation, in matter, the Egyptians spoke of as Maat. In Her cycles and rhythms we see our own. It is a connection that teaches us the natural patterns of change.

For many centuries people in Mexico have told the story of a beautiful woman who came to live in one of the small villages. She lived with the people day by day; she worked, she sang, and she danced with them. And in the evenings, she told them stories, teaching them her ways. She spoke of a time in the light of the new moon — a time to spin and to plant. She spoke of a time in the glow of the full moon, a time to weave and to nurture. She spoke of a time to complete and to harvest, when the moon was on the wane. And she showed them how to go inward, to meditate and to pray — when the moon was dark.

She stayed with the people until they knew her ways, until her ways were their own. Then one season under the full moon light, the people sang and danced, sang and danced, until ecstasy filled the night. In the spinning of sound and movement, the woman flew. She flew in the moonlight — until she *was* Moon.

The people, then, knew her name. She was their relative. Through the seasons and the generations that followed, they looked into the night sky and remembered the teachings of Moon. There is a time for spinning and planting; there is a time for weaving and nurturing and harvesting; and there is a time for going inward to meditate and pray.

THE SPINNING WHEEL

This archetypal moon cycle when related to woman's growth has been described as Maiden, Mother, Crone. Although this is a wheel of three, there is the understanding that all rises from the fourth, the dark womb, the matrix. In his discussion of the sacred syllable "Aum," Joseph Campbell sites a passage from the *Upanishads* that is an echo of the archetypal moon wheel: "Om! This perishable sound is all. It is the Past, the Present, the Future, all that has become, is becoming and is yet to be. Moreover, whatever transcends this three-fold Time — that also is OM."

This sacred syllable AUM (or Om since in Sanskrit "a" and "u" together are pronounced as "o"), says Campbell, is further described in the Upanishads as composed of four "elements" of consciousness. The "a" is the vibration of the waking state; "u" the vibration of the dreaming state, and "m" is deep sleep, intuitive wisdom — "the measure (*miti*), the termination or quenching when all become one." Underlying these three is the fourth, the silence out of which all beginning and ending arise — transcendent, "supremely blissful and without a sound."[10]

In this exercise you take a look at the four archetypal aspects in yourself. Start by some sketching of responses as you reflect on each.

One: The Mirror of Crone (the wisdom to choose and to end)

Amy de Vargas © 1994

What are you ending? What do you need to end? What are you not choosing to do? What holds you back? What are you letting go of in your life? What are you shedding? What is coming to culmination What experiences are you wise from? What truths have come from the compost of your experience?

Two: The Mirror of Matrix (the place of rest and renewal)

Amy de Vargas © 1994

Where do you go to renew your energy? How do you rest? Where do you find comfort? How do you spend your time alone? Where do you find "peace and quiet"? Where do you go when you are "on retreat"?

Three: The Mirror of Maiden (creative impulse, beginnings)

Amy de Vargas © 1994

What is sprouting newly in your life? What new ideas, new projects, work, relationships? What are you creating newly? What do you still feel "awkward" doing? What are you curious about? What are you excited about? What have you done that is a new experience? When do you feel vulnerable?

Four: The Mirror of Mother (Preserver: She who holds us all together)

Amy de Vargas © 1994

What do you have in abundance? What do you give in abundance? Where and when do you feel most full? Most at home? Most happy? What are you accomplished at doing? What has come to fruition for you? What and who do you weave into your life? What do you protect? What would you like to nurture so that it grows larger?

Four Mirrors

1. Draw a mirror for each of your four aspects. In each mirror, collage or draw images that reflect that aspect of yourself.

2. Dwell with your mirrors one at a time. What feelings are evoked by each? Do you have favorites? What qualities, if any, in each do you dislike?

3. Imagine someone close to you looking at the image in each of these mirrors. What reactions, what comments would they make? What qualities do you think they would affirm or acknowledge? What qualities do you think they would be uncomfortable with?

4. Which of the mirror images do you feel most hesitant to bring forward in your relationships. Create a dialogue between this aspect and a person close to you.

 Circle of Four

Draw a circle on a large sheet of paper. Within it, draw or collage images that represent each of your four aspects. (Or create circle within circle.) Allow each to take as much space within the circle as it wants. Dwell with the collage over a period of time, changing it as you are drawn to do so.

 SOUL CIRCLES

Spirals and circles and crosses — these are ancient symbols of change and of balance. Whereas the spiral suggests the polar swings of change, the circle not only suggests the continuity of movement of the spiral but also unity and wholeness. If you were to look at a spiral from above, you would see a series of concentric circles spinning out from one center of origin.

The center of the circle is "the oldest place," yet self-renewing; pouring forth energy, yet ever present. It is the seed essence, the pearl of becoming.[11] Carl Jung called it the "scintilla," or soul spark, the image of Deity unfolding in nature, in the world, and in us.[12] It is the center that prevents the polarities represented by the cross, from splitting asunder, that brings winter back toward spring, activity back toward repose, grief back toward tranquility. If you are on the outer rim of the circle, you will experience being up and being down; in the center, however, the experience is of harmony. Since the ingredients of life are polarities (light and dark; east and west; cold and heat; joy and pain; masculine and feminine) they are always going out of balance. In the natural world, cycles are the means of restoring balance. Jung speculated that the self also has innate ways of restoring balance. He noticed that his clients spontaneously drew what he called "soul circles" especially during periods of stress and disruption in their lives. Although the circles were similar in design and imagery to the "mandalas," meditation circles, of the Hindu tradition, the people who drew them were usually unaware of the connection. They appeared to draw the circles as mirrors of the growth and change happening inside of them — and simply because it felt good to draw them.

Because the circle is reflected around us in so many ways, it is a powerful holographic image. Black Elk's words are still for me the most beautiful description of the circle way:

> *Everything the power of the World does is done in a circle. The sky is round, and I have heard that the earth is round like a ball, and so are all the stars. The wind, in its greatest power, whirls. Birds make their nests in circles, for theirs is the same religion as ours. The sun comes forth and goes down in a circle. The moon does the same, and both are round. Even the seasons form a great circle in their changing and always come back again to where they were. The life of a man is a circle from childhood to childhood, and so it is in everything where power moves. Our tepees were round like the nests of birds, and these were always set in a circle, the nation's hoop, a nest of many nests, where the Great Spirit meant for us to hatch our children.*[13]

We are connected deeply by the circle image — for it is the oldest, most universal image of self; the oldest, most universal image of nature's cycles; and the oldest most universal image of Deity. "From the stationary disk of the Sun God, to the great turning Wheel of the Universe," writes Evelyn Eaton, the circle represents "both the Creator and the Created, where everything in the cosmos finds its appointed place."[14] Drawing circles is, then, both a very ancient and a very contemporary way of finding our at-homeness in our selves and in creation.

 ## Circle Doodling

For a week or so, "doodle" circles. See what comes spontaneously through your hands. At the end of the week, make a collage of the circle designs you have created. Or select one to finish in more detail

Write a description of the circle that most intrigues you. Notice what the description reveals about its imagery and meaning.

THE FOUR

In a story from *Snowy Earth Comes Gliding*, Evelyn Eaton describes the feeling of futility that overcomes her when she tries to find words to describe sacred experience. She is watching a Paiute friend weave four colors — red, white, black, and yellow — into a design. Eaton asks if the colors symbolize the four directions, sensing as she asks that the words were not quite right and probably the question wasn't either. "Something...." her friend replies. The two lapse into a "companionable silence," Eaton says, thinking of "the sacred Four Great Primary Forces, the four servants of the Great Mysterious, who dwell at the four directions...."[15]

Most people identify the Four by earth associations: north, south, east, west; matter, fire, air, water; winter/summer, spring/fall. The qualities of these are then expanded to include our personal experience of body (matter), energy (fire), mind (air), emotions (water). The richness and power of these associations come from a well many thousands of years deep, filled with the memory of life on planet earth, the memory of the turning of sun, moon, and earth.

Our experience of the sun goes far back into primal memory: the memory of the sun's radiance birthing a new day in the east, warming the earth and our bodies; its glow disappearing in the west, bringing darkness, moonlight, and sleep; the changing of the seasons as the sun journeys from north to south, from summer to winter and back again. We are deeply imprinted by these natural cycles. So deeply imprinted, in fact, that Carl Jung describes our knowing of the Four as innate. He observed that his clients not only spontaneously drew circle designs, but that they instinctively divided them into four. He called this repeating archetype "the quaternity," and noted how it recurred in symbolic imagery everywhere.[16]

There are many excellent discussions of the meanings surrounding the Four. It is interesting, however, to look at them from a variety of approaches, for instance a selection such as *The Spiral Dance* by Starhawk, *The Medicine Wheel* by Sun Bear, *The Mother Peace Tarot Book* by Vicki Nobel, *The Wheels of Life* by Anodea Judith, and *Celebrating The Holy-Days* by Waverly Fitzgerald.

You can keep on reading for a long time and never absorb all the meanings surrounding this archetype of the Four Creative Powers. But since the memory is in us, it usually only takes a "seeding" of suggestions to set in motion our own experiencing of them. This is such a seeding:

East; Air, spring, beginnings, sun rise, yellow, light, logos (the word), mind, inspiration, consciousness, clarity, sight, wind, breath, waxing moon, wings, birds, especially eagle.

South; Fire, summer, spirit, creativity, sexual fire, desire, heart flame, full moon, will, power, purification, red, orange, green, lion, cobra, coyote.

West; Water, fall, emotion, womb of creation, fertility, cleansing, waning moon, intuition, the unconscious, sleep, dream, hibernation, blue, black bear, whale, dolphin, fish.

North; Earth, mountain, standing stones, body, winter, wisdom, material gain, money, health, form, disintegration, death, new moon, black, white, cow, bull, bison, wolf, snake.

You can know the Four with your mind by remembering your experience with earth, sun, moon — and your self. You can also know them by simply asking and listening.

 At The Four Gateways

A Journey of Imagination

Be sure you are in a comfortable and uninterrupted space. Breathe, release tension, and ground.

Become aware of which direction you face: East, South, West, North. Listen for a moment to see if you wish to change the way you are facing. Trust impulse. Again breathe and ground. Become aware that you stand before an Elemental Gateway. Feel the fullness of its power. Give thanks for the gifts of this Power, calling them out with words or sounds. With your heart open, ready to receive, ask for the healing gifts it offers. Listen and give thanks.

When you are ready, breathe, ground, and take time to record your experience in words or images.

Listen to your own knowing about how many of these elemental journeys to do at one time and the interval between them. When you are ready, follow this same process with each of the four, allowing impulse to guide you to the directions,. You may find that you do more than one journey in a single direction.

 Visualizing A Mandala of Becoming

A Journey of Imagination

Be sure you are in a comfortable and uninterrupted space. Breathe, release tension, and ground, allowing your roots to go deeply into the earth. See yourself sitting on the earth in a place that is special to you. You sit at the center of a circle. Breathe and feel yourself at the center.

As you sit here in the center, be aware of the larger circle around you: the light from the rising sun in the East illuminates and flows through you. You breathe the inspiration of a new dawning. The sun warms your body as morning gives way to mid-day and spring to summer in the fires of the South. Feel the warmth growing inside you, leaping in the fires of creativity.

As the sun begins to cool into evening, like summer into fall, the mists and rains begin to fall around you. You see the moon appear in the darkening sky, pulling the tides of the oceans, pulling the waters within you. You open to this birthing flow, letting go to the night, letting go to the winter turning. In your body, in your hands, in your voice, you begin to feel the stirring, the life impulse rising to take form, to take shape.

Breathe. Fill yourself with the awareness of being at the center of this circle. As you inhale, feel the powers flowing to the center from the four directions, filling you with the gifts of your creativity. As you exhale, feel the spinning out from the center, the spinning out of your creations.

What are you spinning out in your life right now? What are the main threads you are creating? Notice what they look like. Visualize them spinning out from the center. What color are they:? How strong? What is their texture? How much impulse propels them? How do they move? (as spokes, spirals, circles, waves?)

Continue to breathe in, feeling the inflow of the circle to the center; and to breathe out, watching the outflow of creation. When you are ready, breathe yourself back to present time.

 ### Creating A Mandala of Becoming

A mandala may be created with the intent of keeping it for meditation or it may be given to the natural forces of change. If you are at the beach, for instance, use what you find around you — shells, rocks, plants, feathers — letting impulse lead you to the objects that feel right.

Suggested steps:

1. Draw the circle. Put at the center a symbol for the essential self or the source of becoming.

2. Draw, color, or symbolize the four powers as you experienced them.

3. Draw, color, or symbolize the outflow of creations from the center. Let these "threads" of creation look and move in the way you saw them in your imagining.

4. What colors draw forth and nurture the highest potential of these creations? Let the colors take shape or image.

5. What animals, plants, birds draw forth the strengths of these creations?

 ## RANDOM ACTS

It is November at Wanderland. We race with time to protect the half framed house from the first winter rainstorms. Several days ago I realized that something beautiful had happened: I felt surrounded by acts of kindness. I remembered a bumper sticker I saw recently: "Commit Random Acts of Kindness and Senseless Beauty." For once, I feel like I am living in Bumper Sticker Reality.

Friends come wearing toolbelts and carrying armloads of food and dry wood for the fire. One or two talk the language of construction and have the experience of building, but most just learn. We dig, haul, square, level, saw, nail, cook, tend fire, do dishes, and hot tub together. We share stories and laughter. And are amazed at each others' skill. Dawna has become an expert window framer; John still makes the best stew and builds the warmest fires.

Food keeps appearing in abundance, an autumn harvest on the picnic table of a rainforest. One man, too sick with a cold to join the work party, appears at mid-day bearing a box of homemade cookies. Even the forest animals share in abundance, making nightly raids of the camp, taking everything they can carry — jars of peanut butter, boxes of tea, cartons of eggs. I find their stashes under logs and in stumps, the homes of squirrels, raccoons, and mice.

The house begins to take shape, wrapped in blue tarps stretched across the beams to protect the wooden "bones" of the structure from rain. One night as I carry water up the hill toward camp, it appears as Wander Lodge for the first time. At the top of the hill, I see it lit by a single propane lantern, looming large and beautiful in the blue light. Shadow shapes move inside it, carrying ladders, holding beams, hammering. Later, in the hot tub, friends rub each other's shoulders and tell stories of the hero Flaming Duck who pursues the giant banana slug.

Acts of kindness continue. Too many to name. They are a contagion that swell in and around the stress and sorrow of our lives — the storms take the tarps, leaving the new structure flooded; a young friend fights for her life against leukemia; my father learns he is going blind.

There is no depth, no tension, no drama in writing about what is beautiful. This I was taught years ago in Freshman Composition. It is a lesson that the culture has learned well — the media, movies, and fiction all affirm it, weaving for us a thick cloak of anger, violence, and negativity. And so it grows. The principle is quite simple: what is focused upon grows larger.

Today, I talked for awhile with a woman whose work makes her responsible for the lives of many people. She is a union representative who works long hours in situations of stress and conflict. "I have twelve more years in this job," she said. "I am learning how to enjoy the journey instead of racing to a goal because enjoyment of my life was moving so fast away from me. Last week, instead of taking the freeway to Portland, I took a road through the country side. The trees and the fields were so beautiful.

"What would you do?" she asked me. "How do you handle the stress and the worrying?"

"I have been practicing exactly what you are doing," I said. "I focus on the beauty. I see it. I name it. And I let my heart open in giving-thanks."

It is a simple answer, yet difficult, for negativity becomes a habit — one that receives much support from the culture. Focusing on the beauty does not deny pain, it allows the nurturing balance.

Headlines

For several days watch for random acts of kindness and senseless beauty (including your own). Write headlines for them.

Giving-Thanks Tree

Sketch the outlines of a tree that represents your tree of life. This may be journal size, but consider the possibility of a larger creation, perhaps a mural. For at least a week, "collect" gifts of kindness and give them symbolic form as fruits of the tree.

IT IS TIME TO ACCEPT THE GIFT

Someone asked me recently why this book has seven movements. My first response was "It just happened." It is the way the book grew. This is the truest response I can give, for how can you know a child before you give birth to it? Still, many "reasons" came tumbling out in response to my friend's question. "Too many years of teaching," I think to myself when that happens. In the end (about 15 minutes later) I am sure he had more of an answer than he wanted.

Seven unites four and three, bringing together primary polarities such as earth and spirit, body and soul, doing and knowing, masculine and feminine. It "squares" the circle. The square is composed of 4's (the 4 corners, the cross); it is about form and matter. The circle is composed of 3's (360 degrees) and is about continuity, continuous change, yet cyclic balance. In the *Voyager* Tarot, the Major Arcana Seven is "Chariot," which, like the wheel, represents the law of motion. "Your mind, body, heart, and spirit are constantly moving, running toward their highest possible attainment."[17]

Seven is the number of colors in the rainbow, the radiant bridge between heaven and earth. We are rainbow people — wearing a cloak spun from the rainbow hues of the seven primary chakras. The three chakras of the upper body — crown, brow, and throat — are joined by the bridge of the heart to the three chakras of the lower body — solar plexus, sacral center, and root center. To many Native people, the rainbow means harmony. When the bridge is made, when the polarities are united, healing happens. Perhaps this is why folklore says we find a pot of gold at rainbow's end.

Seven is also a moon cycle number. Fourteen steps in the lunar ladder ascend to the light of the full moon; fourteen steps descend to the dark of the new moon. Four weeks of seven days complete the lunar cycle. Seven is, then, a number of change and movement, an ascending and descending spiral and, at the same time, a number of cyclic balance.

The Spinning Wheel has seven movements for all these "reasons" and for some I still do not know. At the same time, this *is* simply the way it grew. Writing, it seems, is always a surrender to what is happening, which may be very different from what you *think* is going to happen. I knew, for instance, that Movement Seven was about balance and change, but when it came time to write it, I could not. For weeks, I wrote and threw it away; wrote and threw it away — and waited. It would not come. Then I realized that I was not listening. That is, I was not listening to the message I was receiving. "First, you must prepare; you, yourself, must balance," I heard, over and over, as if a voice were speaking inside me.

I started an herbal cleansing program, and for the first time in forty years, gave up drinking coffee. The first day of the cleansing, I felt a dark cloud of toxins filling my body. I literally staggered at my work in the forest, unable to keep my balance. Finally, I quit trying to carry on as usual, bundled myself in a blanket, and lay down on a mossy log. I drifted in an hallucinatory state in and out of consciousness, merging with the log beneath me, watching a ball of light, smaller than the sun, drift across the horizon, seeing animals running through the trees in the bright sunlight. "First there are wings," a voice said, clear as everyday reality. "First there are wings?"

The words had a numinous quality as if they meant something — but what?

A few weeks later, I was part of a weekend healing circle. We were instructed to spend time dwelling with our intent, for each of us would be asked before we ventured into our healing journey. In the hours that I pondered the question, my intent kept changing. So many possibilities, so many needs. Finally, when my turn came, I replied: "To heal my body. To open to the power that is coming through me." The first part was easy. It is acceptable to speak of disease; in fact, disease and the process of healing receive much attention. It is, however, not so acceptable to speak of power, especially your own. Yet, the two intentions were really only one: healing means opening to the power that flows through you. The word "medicine," as Native people persist in reminding Anglo-Americans, does not have to do with drugs but rather with the power that comes from being in balance. Medicine brings what was out of balance (in dis/ease) back into balance.

For me, it had been a long journey to this place of speaking my intent, a journey through cultural imprinting that told me I should be as small as possible and know my place, through relationships that taught me how difficult this was, and most of all, through layer on layer of my own confusion and fear. In the circle, as I spoke of my willingness to accept the gifts given me, the shadow shapes of Self Small swirled around me. Who did I think I was? What would people think? In the moment, it seemed far easier to "apply for disability" than to accept ability. But the intent had been spoken.

That afternoon in the healing circle, I lay on the carpeted floor of a comfortable condominium overlooking the ocean, surrounded by a circle of friends. In my journey, however, I lay on the floor of the Underworld, arms stretched out like some giant bird, and surrendered to the waves of sound that moved through me. Far away, I could hear my cries echoed by the support circle, and farther still, beyond all our voices, the overtones of a music so beautiful I can only describe it as "the sound of the goddess singing." I do not know how long I lay there, with the wind and the song moving through me. I do know that for awhile I saw, as if within myself, a growing luminescence, like a pearl of light, glowing through the darkness.

Later, as I sat in circle dwelling with the experience, two thoughts floated through my mind. I felt like I had experienced "wings." I also remembered a knowing that had come to me somewhere during the journey — it was time to accept the gift. About six years ago, when who I was becoming split the skin of who I was, I lost what I had thought most precious to me. "The goddess will take what is most precious...." I remember reading somewhere. It was not something I wanted to understand. I learned, however, that She does — because it is Hers. Both joy and pain attended the birthing of my spirit during that time, for the dying was deep. The gift that came in that growing time, however, still wore the shrouds of grief.

Sometimes we walk the underworld for a long time; the grief and the pain become so much a part of us and of our bodies that we do not accept the gift that rises from the darkness, a gift born out of the movement of change. I was reminded of Carl Jung's description of the birthing self inspired by a mandala drawn by one of his clients: "The fish is making a whirlpool in the sea of the unconscious, and in its midst the precious pearl is being formed." A similar image appears in a Rig Veda hymn:

Darkness there was, concealed in darkness,
A lightless ocean lost in night.
Then the One, that was hidden in the Shell,
Was born through the power of fiery torment.
From it arose in the beginning love,
Which is the germ and seed of knowing.[18]

The gift of our growing, like the pearl, may be born of turmoil. Still there comes a time when in order for healing to happen, the gift must be accepted. "Nature intends the Grail," writes Joseph Campbell. "Spiritual life is the bouquet, the perfume, the flowering and fulfillment of a human life, not a supernatural virtue imposed upon it."[19] Even so, Campbell's work focuses on the journey, not *to* the grail, because the grail is always there, but the journey of initiation that teaches us to accept the *gift* of the grail.

From this journey of self healing, I began to realize that the seventh movement was not simply about change and balance, but about the power which rises from their dance. Sometimes I think the most important lesson for me to learn is simply to get out of my own way, to let go of the face of ego that associates power with false pride, and to let go of the opposite face of ego that diminishes self with thought-forms of inability. In this sense, power is about allowing yourself to unfold. It is about accepting your abilities.

Marlo Morgan, in *Mutant Message, Downunder*, describes the innocence and ease of Aboriginal people in accepting the gift of their power. After an incredible evening of music making, one man joyously names himself Great Composer. A woman who has the gift of knowing time is called Keeper of Time; another, Sewing Master, another, Story Teller. "It wasn't inflated ego I was observing," Morgan writes. "These are merely people who recognize their talents and the importance of sharing and developing the numerous wonders we are given."[20] In the Aboriginal way of seeing, we are the instruments through which the music of the universe seeks expression.

Cloak of Abilities

The Ancestor whose picture appears on the cover of *The Spinning Wheel* wears a cloak of woven images. Each image is a symbol with holographic echoes through many layers of meaning — mythological, psychological, emotional, sensory. She wears this cloak with pride for it is woven from her abilities, spun from the stuff of her life, and patterned by her wisdom.

A cloak of abilities is a life weaving of the gifts you have been given. Here are two suggested approaches for discovering the images that pattern your cloak. In the first one, you start with the image and allow it to mirror personal meaning. In the second, you start with your life experience and collect the images that have grown from it. Follow what works for you and feel free to invent your own methods.

1. *Dwell with the Ancestral Cloak:* Simply follow the movement of your attention. You may wish to sketch the images that attract you, in order to remember them and also to feel their presence in your hands.

Take time to dwell with each image, learning as much as you can about it. If it is an animal, learn about the animal; if a design, explore its shape and meanings. Be open to allowing the image to change as it merges with you and your experience.

Keep following images until you sense that you have all that you need.

Weave your cloak using whatever medium feels right to you.

2. *Harvesting the Life Territory:* Make a list of the abilities that the universe "plays" through you. Try doing this quickly without censoring or critiquing, although you may wish to add to it later.

List difficult times during your life, giving them code names rather than detailed descriptions. Looking back on each from the eagle's eye view, what qualities, what gifts, what new experience came from the gifts?

Draw or clip images that symbolize the gifts of your life.

Weave the images together as a fabric, choosing whatever medium feels right.

 ## Dwelling With The Cloak

Remember you can "try your cloak on" at anytime in this process to see how it feels and how to alter it. But it is especially important to do this when you have completed the weaving.

Find a comfortable, uninterrupted place. Breathe, release tension, ground. See the cloak lying in front of you, a gift of your mythmaking. When you are ready, pick the cloak up and pull it around you — around your back, across your shoulders, over your heart.

Sit for as long as you like — feeling the power of this cloak. Notice what it looks like — its color, design, and weave.

When you are ready, breathe yourself back. If there are alterations to make in your work, make them.

Place this cloak in a special place to remind you of your medicine power.

An Ending Is A Beginning

Remember that garments can be altered, repaired, remade, or cast off. Grandmother Spider teaches the art. The moon and the snake, they teach the wisdom — of growing within, of shedding skins.

For Circles

AFTERWORDS ONE

ince the material of *The Spinning Wheel* evolved from my work with classes, workshops, and circles, you will find that the exercises not only lend themselves easily to group work but also expand and become deeper with the sharing that happens within a circle. I suspect that you will find, as I have, that play and ritual grow quite naturally from the material.

Play allows spontaneity and trust to grow within a group. It also creates bonding faster than any other method I know. To participate, all that is needed is the innocence of the "child-self." Both play and ritual can bring understanding from the mental realm of concepts to the physical realm of experience. What one knows in one's body goes more deeply, is remembered longer, than what is simply stored in the mind. Both play and ritual "act out" the mythology.

I have collected in this section examples of some of the rituals and games that have evolved in my classes. Perhaps they will seed the growth of your own.

Circle Warm-Ups

I use games such as these at the beginning of the circle, to relax the tension, tune people inwardly, and to teach the naturalness of metaphoric thinking.

"Mood Songs": Have a collection of simple instruments in the center of the circle: rattles, bells, chimes, drums.... Breathe, ground, and tune inwardly. Follow impulse in selecting an instrument. Play a song for yourself, one that reflects how you feel. Your song does not need to please anyone but yourself. Begin moving around the room, playing your song. When you meet someone else, play your song with them in any way you like. When you are ready, return to your place in the circle.

"Mood Animals": Follow your breath, allowing it to focus you inward, letting go of your awareness of others in the circle. Become aware of how your body feels, what movements it wants to make. As much as possible, allow yourself to move, following the impulses of your body.

What animal do your movements remind you of? Accept the first answer. Feel the movements of that animal in your own. If possible, allow yourself to move around the room as the animal.

When you are ready, come back to your place in the circle. Breathe, ground, become aware of others in the circle. Share animal stories.

"Polar Animals": Used in sequence with "Mood Animals," this game gives contrast and often a feeling of balance. Instead of moving into grounding and sharing at the end of "Mood Animals," follow the suggestion: "What animal is opposite to your movement?" Give time for feeling the opposite animal. When ready, come back into circle, breathe and ground. Share animal stories.

"Earth Songs": Have a selection of instruments in the center of the circle. Breathe and ground. See yourself sitting in a place on the earth that is special to you. Choose an instrument. Play a song to this place. As the songs of the group reach fullness, begin calling out the names of the places and what you see there, letting voices and music blend.

"Elemental Songs": Let impulse guide you to one of the four directions: East, South, West, North. Choose an instrument and play your song to that elemental pole. The circle may choose to do this as a round (following a sequence) or all at one time. When the momentum of sound builds, call out the qualities of that direction.

"Mood Scenes": Breathe, ground, tune inward. Be aware of how you feel in this moment. What scene is evoked by the way you feel? (a desert, mountain top, stormy night, sunrise, swamp...) Allow yourself to see the colors and feel the weather of this scene. When you are ready, breathe and come back into awareness of the circle. Time may be taken to sketch or write before sharing landscapes.

"Cornucopia of Color": All that is needed is a special bowl and the suggestion: "Imagine that this bowl overflows with all the colors of the rainbow—purples, reds, oranges, yellows, greens, blues— radiant colors flowing in a never ending abundance. Pass the bowl around the circle, take what colors you wish and dress yourself in them. The taking of the colors is done in silence. When the process is complete, each person, going around the circle, introduces themselves in this fashion: "I am _____, dressed in _____."

Treasure, A Symbol Game

This circle game helps you see how naturally symbols work, and opens you to seeing qualities in yourself that you might not ordinarily recognize. It works well with "Gifts of Your Name," Movement One. All it requires is your child selves and some treasures like small stones, shells, beads, feathers.

Put the treasures on a plate and pass it around the circle. Follow your impulse in taking the one that reminds you in some way of yourself.

Next give yourselves permission to explore the space, as children might a new play area. When you meet another person, greet them, and share your treasure. Describe its special qualities, what you like about it, what makes it unique.

Call the circle back with a chime or a drum. When everyone is back together, take a few minutes to write in your journals: What qualities did you discover in the treasure? Remember now that the treasure reminded you of yourself.

Circle Ritual, A Roll Call

You can use this circle ritual to deepen the process started in "The Name Game" and "Creating Story Lines," Movement One. The word "roll" has a powerful doubleness, naming both our persona or role at the moment, and also the wheel of change itself (past/present/future). A roll is a circular movement. A "roll call" created in circle allows each person to affirm their personal mythology by speaking it.

A circle process might go like this:

1) 20 minutes to play around with naming and story lines; 2) 20 minutes to create a name shield; 3) 20 minutes to share in pairs; and 4) about an hour for the circle roll call (for a circle of ten).

Circle Ritual: First, release tension, ground, and attune to center. A simple breathing exercise is a natural way to begin: on the inbreath, filling with light: on the outbreath, releasing tension down through the body into earth.

Join hands as a circle and take a moment to breathe and feel the unity of the circle. Each person then speaks "who they call themselves." You may also wish to add all or part of your initial story line. Notice how your body feels and whether your voice comes from your body, so that you feel what you are saying. You can help each other here, by asking for a repeat of what was said so you can feel its impact more powerfully. Frequently this helps the feeling grow stronger in the speaker. It is not necessary to tell another how they sound: ("You sound like you don't believe it.") This may actually inhibit the speaker.

It is important to notice that in this ritual you are not only gaining confidence in your present persona, but you are also allowing each person to be present without correction or evaluation. To speak the language of your soul's journey takes trust.

Essential Child Game: "Following Impulse"

This game may be used before the "Essential Child" journey of Movement Three to help tune people back to spontaneous response. Many have forgotten the joy of simply following impulse in play. The game reminds you of this child-like place.

The rules are simple: you have permission to explore and play as your impulse guides you. In it an exercise in "listening" and "allowing." You need, of course, a safe, interesting place (this could be either inside or outside). You may wish to create this space by adding interesting things. The attic, for instance, is filled with mobiles, masks, musical instruments, pictures, paper, chalk, books, some simple toys (like a kaleidoscope), stones and shells.... You also need to suspend self consciousness.

You might agree to come back to circle with the sounding of a chime or drum. The circles I have played with have become so absorbed in exploring that they "forget" time.

Eight Precious Things

When I came across this list of "eight precious things," I was intrigued. The list read as follows: a book, coin, mirror, pearl, artemisia leaf, jade gong, musical lozenge, and rhinoceros horn.[1] I decided to play with this list in the class I was teaching on "Balance and Change" (Movement Seven) and see what happened.

I drew a symbol for each of the gifts on small pieces of paper and placed them face down in the center of the circle.

"There are eight precious gifts in the center of the circle," I said. "Follow impulse in choosing one. Since it comes from a list of eight, be open to the possibility that your gift tells you something about balance." Then we spent some time dwelling with our gift — imagining that we held it, exploring it in any way we desired.

When the circle was ready, we began moving around the attic, like children at play, following impulse. When we met, we greeted each other and shared something about the gift we had been given. The moving and sharing complete, we came once more into circle where each of us spoke of our gift and its meaning for us.

Mandala Ritual

This ritual evolved from circle play with Sheila Broun's mandala symbolizing the wheel of change (Movement Seven, p. 107).

First lay out the mandalic lines, using four pieces of heavy string or rope about six to eight feet long. Create the mandala on the directional axis: Winter Solstice in the North; Summer Solstice in the South; Spring Equinox, East: Fall Equinox, West. Use a special crystal, stone, or shell to mark the center. Write out the meanings of all eight poles on slips of paper (Samhain: she dies; Winter Solstice: she turns, and so on).

There are eight positions; however, two people can hold one pole, or one person can hold two adjacent poles, if the circle is smaller or larger than eight.

First movement: Tell people to find their place in the circle by following impulse (rather than calling attention to the meaning of the poles).

Breathe and ground as a circle. Pick up the end of the string in front of you and the slip of paper with the pole's meaning.

Starting with where you are in seasonal cycle (Winter Solstice, Spring Equinox...) begin the chant. Each person says the meaning of the pole they hold. Go around and around the circle, listening to the turning of the wheel. When the chant is well established, you might try adding a simple step to the left to turn the circle wheel as you listen to the cycle.

Second movement: At the end of a complete cycle, the circle moves clockwise, and each person assumes a new pole. If time allows, let each person experience the full movement (eight poles) of integrated solar/lunar turning.

Third movement: Play the polarities. Again starting with where you are seasonally, one person speaks the polarity and is answered by the person at the opposite pole (at the other end of the string). Do this several times; then reverse order. For example, "She turns" (Winter Solstice); "She shines" (Summer Solstice). Reversed: "She shines"; "She turns." Reversal helps you let go of positive/negative and linear sequence, and allows you a deeper sense of the polar dynamic.

Twelve Ways to Surf Emotion
AFTERWORDS TWO

1. Breathe. The natural inflow, outflow of breath cleanses the body and helps us to let go of tension, of emotion. Joanna Macy teaches a simple breath she calls "breathing through" that not only helps release emotion as it comes up from memory of past experience, but also helps you to stay sensitive and responsive to present experience without storing the pain in your body. It goes like this:

    Relax. Center on your breathing. Visualize your breath as a stream flowing up through your nose, down through windpipe, lungs. Take it down through your lungs and, picturing an opening in the bottom of your heart, out through that hole to reconnect with the larger web of life around you. Let the breath-stream, as it passes through you, appear as one loop with the vast web, connecting you with it...keep breathing.

    Breathe in the pain (or whatever you are feeling) like a dark stream, up through your nose, down through your trachea, lungs, and heart and out again into the world net.... You are asked to do nothing for now, but let it pass through and out again, don't hang on to the pain. Surrender it to the healing resources of life's vast web."

    Despair and Empowerment in The Nuclear Age, Joanna Macy

2. Free write in your journal. Don't censor. Let whatever comes out, come out. Remember that it may not be in words.

3. Write a dialogue with your emotion. This process not only distances you from the emotion it often gives you insight into it. To do this, you simply name the emotion; speak to it as if it separate from you; then let it answer. Follow first impulse on this. Don't try to figure it out. Let the dialogue continue as long as there is momentum behind it.

4. If the emotion arises from an interaction with someone in your past, write a letter in your journal or dialogue with them.

5. Use sound. Breathe, find the place in your body where you feel the emotion. Inhale, allow a sound to move through this place on the exhale. Inhale and again sound and exhale through the place in your body where you feel the emotion.

6. Use dance or movement to express the emotion.

7. Make a mask that represents the emotion you are feeling. Dance or act out the feeling with the mask.

8. If you are releasing anger, try a plastic bat and a big pillow — and let fly.

9. If you are feeling grief or sorrow, try curling up with a large soft pillow, holding it close to your center.

10. Water cleansing: You will need a safe space where you can make whatever sounds

you wish. Place a bowl of water in front of you (you may wish to use sea salt or crystals in the water). Breathe and ground. Allow yourself time to come into your body and to feel your emotion. Breathe and release the emotion with sound, seeing it in your mind's eye, propelled into the cleansing water. As it hits the water, see it transform into light. Continue the process until you feel it is completed. Give the water back to the earth.

If you do not wish to go into the emotion, respect that. Shift focus.

11. Let the earth heal you. Go for a walk in the forest, or by the ocean, or listen to the birds singing in your back yard.

12. Go biking, or walking, or running, or swimming, or take a luxurious bath. Nurture yourself.

Always honor your own timing, your own rhythms, that you grow in your own way. At the same time, honor emotions for they are teachers—teachers of what it is to be alive and sensitive in body; teachers of what it is to respond to experience. Through emotion, we learn what we can and cannot do. We learn what situations are nurturing to us and what ones are not. We learn what we wish to choose and what we wish to change.

Inner Dance by Diane Mariechild is an excellent self help book for journeying into emotion with breath and active imagination. In addition, Joanna Macy's *Despair and Empowerment in The Nuclear Age*, is invaluable in teaching how to reclaim both our sensitivity and our personal power. For journaling exercises that allow you to explore emotion see Tristine Rainer's *New Diary*.

Surfing

> If I could remember
>   to be a surfer
>   riding the tides of emotion
>   feeling as I go
>
> If I could remember
>   to be a surfer-
>   feel, breathe,
>   and let go
>
> I could be
>   surfing feeling
>   as I grow
>   feeling as I grow.
>   gwendolyn

Notes

ACKNOWLEDGEMENT

1. Frank Waters, *Book of the Hopi,* 1963.
2. Barbara Walker, *Woman's Encyclopedia of Myths and Secrets,* 1983, p. 957.

MOVEMENT ONE:

1. Diane Wolkstein and Samuel Noah Kramer, *Inanna,* 1983, p. 5.
2. Clarissa Pinkola Estes, *Women Who Run With The Wolves,* 1992, p. 95.
3. Wolkstein and Kramer, *Inanna,* p. 68.
4. Walker, pp. 221—224.

MOVEMENT TWO

1. Maria von Franz, *Time,* 1978, p. 32.
2. Ralph Blum, *The Book of Runes,* 1932, p. 111.
3. von Franz, Plate 2, *"Oceanus."*
4. von Franz, pp. 66-67.
5. Joseph Campbell, *Historical Atlas of World Mythology, Vol II: The Way of the Seeded Earth,* Part One: "The Sacrifice," frontspiece.
6. Wolkstein and Kramer, *Inanna.*
7. Marija Gimbutas, *The Language of the Goddess,* 1989, pp. 265-266.
8. Meinrad Craighead, *The Mother's Songs,* 1986, "Garden," p. 53.

MOVEMENT THREE

1. Craighead, *The Mother's Songs,* "Journey," p. 71.
2. von Franz, *Time,* plate 5.
3. Evelyn Eaton, *Snowy Earth Comes Gliding,* 1974, p. 52.
4. Susan Strauss, *Coyote Stories,* 1991.
5. Wolkstein, *Inanna,* p. 180.
6. Barbara Walker, *The Woman's Encyclopedia of Myths and Secrets,* 1983.
7. Buffie Johnson, *Lady of the Beasts,* 1988, p. 194.
8. Anodea Judith, *Wheels of Light,* 1989, p. 68.

MOVEMENT FOUR

1. Ralph Blum, *The Book of Runes,* 1932, p. 11.
2. Walker, p. 93.
3. Meinrad Craighead, *The Litany of the Great River,* 1991, p. 13.
4. Anne Cameron, *Daughters of Copper Woman,* 1981, p. 123
5. Cameron, p. 54.
6. William Brandon, *The Magic World,* 1971, pp. 102-103.

MOVEMENT FIVE

1. Joseph Campbell, *The Power of Myth,* 1988, p.198.
2. Thomas Sanders and Walter Peek, eds., *The Literature of The American Indian,* 1976, p. 22.
3. Joseph Campbell, *The Way of the Animal Powers,* Part 2: "Mythologies of the Great Hunt," 123-136.

5. Gloria Levitas, Frank Vivelo, Jacqueline Vivelo, eds., *American Indian Prose and Poetry,* 1974, p. 102.
6. Eaton, p. 35.
7. Eaton, p. 43-45.
8. Waters, *Book Of The Hopi,* p. 7.
9. Waters, pp. 4-5.
10. David Spangler, *The Laws Of Manifestation.*

MOVEMENT SIX

1. Monica Sjoo and Barbara Mor, *The Great Cosmic Mother,* 1975, p. 56.
2. Wolkstein and Kramer, *Inanna,* p. 29ff.
3. *Inanna,* p. 51ff.
4. *Inanna,* p. 156.
5. Estes, *Women Who Run With The Wolves,* p. 29.
6. *Inanna,* p. 59.
7. *Inanna,* p. 64.
8. Walker, *Woman's Encyclopedia of Myths and Secrets,* p. 326.
9. Walker, p. 366.
10. Walker, p. 70.
11. Walker, *The Woman's Dictionary of Symbols and Sacred Objects,* p. 69.

MOVEMENT SEVEN

1. Cameron, pp. 19-20.
2. Video recording, *Green On Thursday,* produced in Albuquerque, New Mexico, 1986.
3. *Inanna,* p. 21.
4. *Inanna,* p. 24.
5. Blum, *Book Of The Runes.*
6. Walker, *Encyclopedia,* p. 560.
7. Walker, p. 561
8. Bill Mollison, *Permaculture: A Practical Guide for a Sustainable Future,* 1990, p. 2.
9. Susan Seddon Boulet, *Shaman,* 1989.
10. Joseph Campbell, THE WAY OF THE ANIMAL POWERS, Part 2: *Mythologies of the Great Hunt,* IX.
11. Jose and Mriam Arguelles, *Mandala,* 1972, p. 60.
12. Carl Jung, *Mandala Symbolism,* 1973, p. 5.
13. John Niedhardt, *Black Elk Speaks,* 1961.
14. Eaton, p. 43ff.
15. Eaton, p. 33.
16. Jung, *Mandala Symbolism.*
17. James Wanless, *Voyager Guidebook,* 1986.
18. Jung, p. 19.
19. Campbell, *Power Of Myth,* p. 20.
20. Marlo Morgan, *Mutant Message, Downunder,* 1993, p. 97.

AFTERWORDS ONE

1. Walker, *Dictionary,* p. 68.